Although the great Chartist meeting and petition of 1848 have been written about many times before, Catherine Howe sets this story in its wider context, She brings a fresh eye to the material, weighing things up at a distance from the debates that have preoccupied professional historians. Howe is a story teller and what this book offers is a straightforward, detailed and open-minded account of what happened in that year.

Stephen Roberts
Research School of Humanities and the Arts
Australian National University

LONDON STORY 1848

CHARTISTS, CONFEDERATES, REVOLUTIONARIES

CATHERINE HOWE

APS BOOKS
STOURBRIDGE

APS Books,
4 Oakleigh Road,
Stourbridge,
West Midlands,
DY8 2JX

APS Books is a subsidiary of
the APS Publications imprint

www.andrewsparke.com

Cover photograph of Kennington Common demonstration by William Edward Kilburn 1818-1891
Frontispiece cartoon Alfred Pearse 1855-1933

ISBN 9781789960853

AUTHOR'S NOTE

Writing of today's Britain, Angela Eagle and Imran Ahmed say in their *The New Serfdom*: 'When so many feel their basic needs and wants are being denied, it's not hard to see where the inchoate, latent anger that is driving our political volatility comes from. When people feel the rich have lived it too large and left so little for their fellow citizens, there comes a time of political revolution.' It seems to me pertinent to set side-by-side this view of today's Britain with the Britain of 1848 for it so well describes our society back then.

The events which occurred in London in 1848 have already been thoroughly researched and recorded by David Goodway, *London Chartism 1838-1848*, and John Saville, *1848, The British State and the Chartist Movement*. These books have enabled me to write this simple telling of the story of that year from what might be called the ground up. I mean to offer here a small window, howsoever dust-laden, on the individuals who found themselves caught up in the events of 1848 and to give some sense of what they might have thought and felt through what can be gleaned from government papers, parliamentary reports, letters, biographies, memoirs, journals and newspaper reportage. Anger and frustration are the emotions which characterise one side, fear the other. I find that my view of the way in which the events of this significant year played themselves out departs in one particular from those of many eminent Chartist historians. The predominant view is that Chartism was never an insurrectionary organisation. I could not help but conclude that in 1848 the National Charter Association did act as an insurrectionary organisation, albeit briefly. And so, with this caveat in mind, I hope these pages give a useful telling of the events of 1848 to any who read them.

Catherine Howe
March 2020

i

LONDON STORY 1848

CONTENTS

PART ONE

1842-1848

1
London 1848

In the bitter cold of early February 1848 Londoners first heard news from Italy of Lombardy and Venetia's expulsion of Austrian troops from their provinces. For thirty years Austria had occupied northern Italy and now daily reports of the Italian rising came into London from Paris with unprecedented speed through the telegraph service. Austria 'fears that Italy will understand them and rise as one man to respond to the call' printed the *Northern Star* while *The Times* assured its readers that 'The power of Austria to crush any popular movement attempted in the states has at no time been doubted'[1] London's colonies of Italians, Irish, French, Germans, Poles reading these reports would wonder if this was the start of something. Three weeks later revolutionaries took Paris and as more continental countries rose against their rulers, suddenly the future looked malleable.

While Italy and France were thus engaged, a Londoner called John James Bezer, thirty-one years old, known familiarly as Monops because he was blind in his left eye (from having contracted smallpox when a baby), was mixing with the political radicals of London's East End where he lived and worked as a street-seller of fish. He had been born in Spitalfields in 1816 to Mary, a cotton winder, and James, an ex-navy man turned barber. By the time he was nine years old he and his mother were on the streets of London's East End selling hot cross buns, unsuccessfully, so he became an errand boy for a warehouseman in Newgate Street. When the errand work ended, he helped out at his Sunday School on Raven Row until taking up employment as a chemist's assistant in a corner shop on Jewin Street. By the time he was a teenager he was working as an assistant to a grocer down in Camberwell, work which he enjoyed, but family difficulties brought him back to his mother, still living in Whitechapel. There he started making shoes, though not trained for it, before gaining employment as a bookbinder's porter. In the late 1830s, when a young married man, he descended into the dim world of street begging. James Bezer was so ashamed of this necessity that each day he took himself across the river into Surrey, as far away as

Brixton village, to practice the occupation of street-singer in the hope that no-one there would recognise him. By his early twenties he had grown rebellious against authority. By 1848 he was thinking of revolution. The newspaper reports of the risings in Sicily, Italy and France in February 1848 would have beeen a great encouragement to him.[2]

Some three miles to the west of James Bezer, a lawyer named James Macnmara was sitting in his rooms on Cleveland Row, behind The Mall, waiting for clients. Few came. He was young, inexperienced and lacking useful contacts. Little did he know in early February 1848 that the reports of risings on the Continent heralded a time, not far off, when he would have more than enough work to occupy him. Ten minutes' walk south of James Macnmara, at Chesham Place, Lord John Russell the British Whig Prime Minister would contemplate the same newspaper reports in a very different light from the fish-seller Bezer or the lawyer Macnmara. There was pressing reason for any unease he and his Home Secretary George Grey might feel at news of continental uprisings. The revolutionary provinces of northern Italy were ruled from Vienna, Ireland was ruled from London, and in Ireland unrest was increasing. Prosecutable offences in Ireland had doubled in the last three years; years in which Ireland had faced a protracted and appalling famine.[3] In response, George Grey brought in a Crimes and Outrages Act in an attempt to stop attacks in Ireland on landowners and their livestock. In London there were already many Irish, and revolutions on the Continent would be an encouragement to Irish nationalists everywhere to fight for repeal of the Act of Union which in 1801 had swept away Ireland's own parliament.[4]

To add to the British government's unease, the National Charter Association, which for the past ten years had campaigned for parliamentary reform, was about to convene at the Literary & Scientific Institute on John Street by Tottenham Court Road. Its plan; to present a People's Charter calling for political reforms backed by a great petition signed, it was claimed, by five million British working people. Only one in every seven men in Britain had the vote, and the possibility of a vote for women was beyond sensible contemplation. The National Charter Association's

'People's Charter' of 1848 called for a vote for all free men over the age of twenty-one, so that laws affecting the lives of everyone would be fashioned by the voice of every man. But what so exercised the Whig government and its majority in parliament was that the National Charter Association had at last succeeded in drawing the Irish Nationalist Confederates into an alliance. The Confederates would support the Chartist call for parliamentary reform, the Chartists would support the Confederate call for Repeal of the Union. This alliance was a great threat to the Whig government and those it represented. To the ruling classes in London the threat of insurrection in Ireland was a real and dreadful one and something altogether different from the home-grown Chartist threat. This, combined with continental revolutionary events, made the propertied classes of London very apprehensive indeed.

Six months earlier, a member of the National Charter Association speaking from the heights of Blackstone Edge, a spectacular outcrop of stone which looks out over mile upon mile of east Lancashire, had urged a crowd of Lancashire and Yorkshire working people to raise the petition to back the People's Charter. The speaker was thirty-four-year-old Peter Murray McDouall, a Scot, a medical doctor, ardent of temperament, sparkling-eyed, and with fair hair long enough that he must push it behind his ears.[5] He was a long-standing Chartist and had only recently returned to England with his wife and young children after self-imposed exile in Paris to avoid arrest by the British authorities. At Blackstone Edge he urged the preparation of a petition in support of the People's Charter. The two previous petitions of 1839 and 1842 had impressed the socialists in France and had raised the British Chartist cause to such prominence there that he believed the Association should petition again.

And so, in the following months what would be the great 1848 Chartist petition was signed by those millions of working people in time-honoured fashion, on hillsides and in fields, in streets and squares, meeting rooms and lecture halls. Its sheets would be taken to London, stuck together, made into enormous rolls and then carried to the Houses of Parliament by a great crowd of supporters. No-one anticipated that at the very time of its presentation to parliament at Westminster the Continent would be in the throes of revolution.

The day on which news of the successful French revolution hit London, Friday 25th February 1848, a colleague of Peter McDouall, George Julian Harney, was so exultant that he upset a fruit seller's stall as he ran from Charing Cross to tell his émigré friends living in Soho of the wonderful event.[6] Revolution in France signified something much as a starting gun does. It represented the chance of great social change everywhere and Julian Harney had been waiting a long time for it. When James Bezer was struggling as a street beggar in the late 1830s, the fiery young Harney had worn the red cap of the 1789 French Revolution, had wielded a dagger, had urged action upon the first Chartist Convention of 1839, held in London, later Birmingham, believing that the only way to persuade government to enact the People's Charter was through insurrection. Since then he had seen attempted British risings and one great national strike, none of which had resulted in full-blooded revolution. Julian Harney now doubted that the British would ever be sufficiently inclined to depose their rulers through risings as the Parisians were but when news of the French Revolution of 1848 reached London, he seems to have allowed himself a brief belief in the imminence of change. The terms of the People's Charter could become reality after all.

The British parliament was astounded at the news from France. When the people had raised the barricades and taken to the streets of Paris on 23rd February, support from the National Guard had, within hours, put the Parisian revolutionaries in a position of power 'with not the slightest idea how to govern,' said one English commentator.[7] Alphonse de Lamartine now presided over a Provisional Government in Paris while Louis Blanc led the socialist camp within that government and succeeded in establishing a Ministry of Labour and Progress to oversee workers' conditions; the dynamics between Lamartine, conservative in his politics, and Louis Blanc's Socialists would play themselves out in following months.

In London, the Whig Prime Minister John Russell assured parliament that his government would not interfere in any way with France's internal affairs. No, the main concern was in what manner this revolution would affect dissidents at home: the Chartists and Irish Confederates. In Ireland, news of the Paris rising came to the Confederates 'like a message from heaven.'[8] In the House of Lords it produced great apprehension which was made worse by evidence received from Dublin of openly declared revolutionary intent.

On Thursday 24th February, Lord Stanley read out loud to his fellows in the House of Lords from the *United Irishman*, a paper produced by John Mitchel, young Irish lawyer and journalist. In it Mitchel placed a letter to 'The Right Hon. The Earl of Clarendon, Englishman; calling himself her Majesty's Lord Lieutenant General and General Governor of Ireland:

'My Lord...the sway of your nation here is drawing near its latter days...An exact half-century has passed away since the last holy war waged in this island, to sweep it clear of the English name and nation. And we differ from the illustrious conspirators of [1798], not in principle—no, not an iota—but, as I shall presently show you, materially as to the mode of action. Theirs was a secret conspiracy—ours is a public one...In plain English, my Lord Earl, the deep and irreconcilable disaffection of this people to all British laws, law-givers, and law-administrators, shall find a voice. That holy hatred of foreign dominion which nerved our noble predecessors fifty years ago...still lives, thank God! and glows as fierce and hot as ever. To educate holy hatred, to make it know itself, and avow itself, and at last fill itself full, I hereby devote the columns of the United Irishman.' [9]

When writing of 'the last holy war' John Mitchel was calling down the spirit of the Irish rebellion of 1798. A leading rebel of 1798, Arthur O'Connor, was alive still and living in France and as it so happened, his nephew, Feargus O'Connor, was now leader of the Chartist movement and living in London. Feargus O'Connor had worked with Peter McDouall and Julian Harney for many years. In all weathers they had stood together upon numberless hustings calling for the terms of the Charter, they had suffered arrest and imprisonment, and they had threatened that physical force brought against them by the authorities would be met with the same. Now they were planning a huge demonstration of working-class strength to accompany the Chartist petition to the Houses of Parliament. What could be more threatening to the authorities than that? And at what a time for it to be unfolding, with revolution across the Channel and violent unrest in Ireland.

2
The Silence (Ireland 1845-1848)

1848 opened in London to freezing temperatures and an influenza epidemic. The streets around Spitalfields, where James Bezer lived, were occupied by families with undernourished children and elderly clinging to the remnants of a hard life. The buildings here housed sometimes forty people under one roof and viral infections would go through these communities like wild fire. There was the fear of cholera too, but that horror would not materialise until the year's end.

London had a population of some two million. The many thousands living in cellars, crowded and decrepit houses and workhouses of the metropolis had been too long demoralised to apply themselves to political matters. Yet the more determined, those like James Bezer and his associates, were likely supporters of Chartism.

For ten years it had been the people of Wales, the Midlands and the industrial north who had faced the soldiers in the expectation of some response from Westminster's politicians to calls for political reform. London's relative peacefulness had been a comfort to the authorities during the Chartist disturbances and trades' strikes of the past decade because no amount of risings in towns like Newport or Merthyr Tydfil, Manchester, Sheffield or Bradford could succeed without London. The Chartist leadership now focused its efforts on the capital. With France risen, would they attempt their own rising when they presented their great petition to parliament in April? The upper and middle classes of London certainly feared so. Working men and Chartists like James Bezer, Soho tailor William Cuffay, George Bridge Mullins a surgeon's apprentice, and bricklayer Joseph Richie later planned for it, as did Peter McDouall. Their leader, Feargus O'Connor, did not.

By 1848, Feargus O'Connor was a gaunt, rangy man, his reddish hair turned grey, and as ambitious now as he had been fifteen years earlier when first entering parliament for County Cork. He had only recently regained a seat in parliament and now represented Nottingham. O'Connor had long agitated for repeal of the Act of

Union between England and his native Ireland and had hoped, for nearly as long, for an Irish alliance with the English, Scottish and Welsh working people. The Irish organisation most suited to Chartism, the Irish Confederation, had rebuffed all O'Connor's overtures but in the months leading up to 1848 he could see his great desire coming to realisation. John Mitchel, in Dublin, was calling for civil disobedience against London's rule while the Confederates, at last, were open to the idea of cooperation with the English Chartists. Mitchel, thirty-one years old, had been a Confederate member until he fell out with its leadership because of his openly revolutionary views.

The Confederates had emerged from the Young Irelanders who, until the close of 1846, had been part of the Dublin-based Repeal Association led by Ireland's 'Great Liberator' Daniel O'Connell; a great liberator of Catholics from their political disabilities but never to be liberator of Ireland from England. The split between the Young Irelanders and Daniel O'Connell's Repeal Association had come about because O'Connell had gambled Repeal of the Union upon a parliamentary alliance with England's Whig party: the party of the present prime minister Lord John Russell, the party of the rising middle-classes, the party which the working classes felt had betrayed them, the party which had just brought in the coercive Crimes and Outrages Act for Ireland and which had no intention of considering Repeal of the Union no matter how strongly O'Connell might hope; the party which, from its London offices, now presided over the course of one of the deepest and most prolonged famines Ireland had ever known.

Hunger was a condition with which Irish cottier, Lancashire industrial worker and London's abject poor were fearfully familiar, but the Irish cottiers were different. They had absolutely nothing but their potato crops upon which to live while the rest of Britain's poor did have bread. When it was heard in 1845 that the potato blight had reached Ireland, it was apparent to everyone that the Irish would starve. The government of the day, Robert Peel's Tory government, set up a Relief Commission in Dublin to manage the awaited famine, and when Peel's government fell in July 1846 John Russell's Whig government took over. It is calculated that in 1846 exported grains from Ireland exceeded imports by 485,000 tons.[10] 'The beef, the mutton, the pork, the grain crops – indeed, everything except the potatoes, had to be sold, and the proceeds paid over to the landlords for rent.'[11] Some say the exported grains would have been of no practical use to cottiers whose cooking facilities and skills were limited to the preparation of potatoes but the fact is that people dying for want of food watched as foodstuffs were shipped out.

John Mitchel saw the results of the first full year of famine for himself as he travelled across Ireland from Dublin to Galway in January 1847:

'In the depth of winter we travelled to Galway, through the very centre of that fertile island, and saw sights that will never wholly leave the eyes that beheld them: cowering wretches, almost naked in the savage weather, prowling in turnip-fields, and endeavouring to grub up roots which had been left, but running to hide as the mail-coach rolled by; very large fields, where small farms had been "consolidated", showing dark bars of fresh mould running through them, where the ditches had been levelled; groups and families, sitting or wandering on the high-road, with failing steps and dim, patient eyes, gazing hopelessly into infinite darkness; before them, around them, above them, nothing but darkness and despair; parties of tall, brawny men, once the flower of Meath and Galway, stalking by with a fierce but vacant scowl; as if they knew that all this ought not to be, but knew not whom to blame, saw none whom they could rend in their wrath; for Lord John Russell sat safe in Chesham Place, and Trevelyan, the grand commission and *factotum* of the pauper-system, wove his webs of red tape around them from afar. So cunningly does civilization work! Around those farmhouses which were still inhabited were to be seen hardly any stacks of grain; it was all gone;...and sometimes, I could see, in front of the cottages, little children leaning against a fence when the sun shone out – for they could not stand – their limbs fleshless, their bodies half-naked, their faces bloated yet wrinkled, and of a pale, greenish hue – children who would never, it was too plain, grow up to be men and women. I saw Trevelyan's claw in the vitals of those children; his red tape would draw them to death; in his Government laboratory he had prepared for them the typhus poison.'[12]

A British officer said of the same western area, '…I confess myself unmanned by the extent and intensity of the suffering…I am a match for anything else I may meet with here, but this I cannot stand…' [13]

The Trevelyan to whom John Mitchell refers was Charles Edward Trevelyan of the British Treasury, working from Whitehall. Trevelyan was a civil servant who had served under Peel's Tory government. His minister now was Sir Charles Wood, Whig Chancellor of the Exchequer, and together they guided an English policy which sought disengagement from responsibility for Ireland. In 1846 an infamous letter was written by Trevelyan to the Commissary General in Ireland advising closure of relief operations: 'Whatever may be done hereafter, these things should be stopped now, or you run the risk of paralysing all private enterprise and having this country on you for an indefinite number of years.'[14]

William Smith O'Brien, an Irish MP who would figure large in the story to come, railed at the Exchequer's policy which required Ireland 'to depend only on her own efforts,' failing which British government ministers were expected to 'resign themselves to…beholding masses of the population of Ireland dying for want of food.'[15]

And so there it was, an Ireland starving and riven with fever; great numbers of her people dying on the streets or in fields or in the workhouses. One million died this way, one million began to make their escape over the Atlantic to New York or over the St George Channel to Liverpool. It is calculated that an average of three hundred people disembarked daily at New York from Ireland in these famine years. Close to one third of a million people arrived at Liverpool in 1847 alone, and many would travel on to London to join family members already there, or to strike out on their own.[16]

The Irish population of London swelled tremendously. 'Ireland! Ireland! That cloud in the west, that coming storm,' prophetically wrote William Gladstone, then a young politician.[17] The Duke of Wellington, now nearly eighty years old, understood the situation well as he had spent much of his childhood at Dangan Castle, County Meath, the same property in which Feargus O'Connor, as a boy, had lived with his family. When famine strikes, Wellington wrote, 'there is no relief or mitigation, excepting recourse to public money. The proprietors of...[Ireland] are amusing themselves in the Clubs in London...and the government are made responsible for the evil, and they must find the remedy for it where they can.'[18]

In London in 1848, the British prime minister Lord John Russell led a government which was disengaged from acting for Ireland except through various coercion Acts in response to agitation. Some years earlier, Russell had written: 'I wish I knew what to do to help [Ireland]...but, as I do not, it is of no use giving her smooth words...and I must be silent.'[19]

3
The Blind Eye (England 1845-1848)

The potato murrain visited the European Continent before descending upon Ireland in 1845; the poor in Europe were hungry and all classes dissatisfied. The weavers in German Silesia attempted an uprising which was put down by King Frederick William IV's Prussian army. In Austria, the ageing Prince Metternich's popularity was waning amongst the liberal middle ground. In Italy the nationalists in the ten states of the peninsula were dreaming of freedom from Austria while their leaders Guiseppe Mazzini and Guiseppe Garibaldi waited in exile, Mazzini in London, Garibaldi in Montevideo. In France, King Louis Philippe was three years away from his February 1848 deposition and Louis Napoleon, nephew of Napoleon Bonaparte, having already attempted to raise a *coup d'état* against the French king, was imprisoned in the French fortress of Ham.

In London in 1845, as long you were not one of the abject poor without the clothing necessary to be seen on the streets, you could go about and enjoy Regent's Park, or Victoria Park in Bethnal Green, both recently opened to the public. You had the Thames upstream from the city to row on, swim in and fish from, you had fairgrounds, menageries, pleasure gardens and you had the theatres at sixpence a time. George Julian Harney, then twenty-eight years old, had a passion for the Shakespeare plays which were being performed in their entirety for the first time in many decades, not only at the patented Haymarket, Drury Lane and Covent Garden theatres but in the smaller theatres too. In 1845 Harney was already sub-editor of Feargus O'Connor's *Northern Star,* and the *Star*'s presses pounded away in Great Windmill Street, close-by London's major theatres where politicians of every hue would go to greenroom gatherings after performances; where, at the Haymarket, Feargus O'Connor's friend, the actress Louisa Nisbett often played; where Lucy Vestris, manager of the Strand's Lyceum Theatre and once lover of O'Connor's friend and political colleague Thomas Slingsby Duncombe, had her theatre redecorated in white, pink and blue, and with gas light to show off all its beauties.

All this was far removed from the hardships endured on the tenanted estates of Ireland, in the cotton and woollen mills of Lancashire and Yorkshire, in the coal mines and foundries of South Wales and the Midlands, and in London's own back streets. Even so, Britain was described by one of Austria's liberals as, 'the most glorious creation of God and nature and simultaneously humanity's most admirable work of art,' which, relatively speaking, was a credible comment.[20] Britain was not too militaristic, was not reigned over by an absolutist monarch or controlled by men of the likes of Austria's Prince Metternich, and chose not to execute its dissenters in too barbaric a fashion – generally it transported them for a few years before issuing a pardon. This was a reputation of which British politicians and the Crown were keenly aware and eager to keep. Britain was nowhere nearly as viscerally repressive as the continental countries but the working people of England, Scotland and Wales, and the cottiers of Ireland fared no better in their daily lives than their fellows across the Channel.

In 1845 a young man called Ernest Jones, born and brought up in the German state of Holstein, was living west of London and had approached Lucy Vestris at the Lyceum Theatre with scripts, but had been rejected by her and others. He needed patronage badly because although a lawyer by training he, like James Macnmara, was finding it hard to make ends meet. In fact, he was bankrupt. He says it was his habit to walk into London from his home with 'a dagger and crabtree stock' upon him, for fear of being seized and carried off to a debtors' prison.[21] He was still in his mid-twenties when, in the New Year of 1846, he made the acquaintance of Chartist Thomas Martin Wheeler. Soon he was calling in at the *Northern Star* offices on Great Windmill Street where he met Julian Harney and where he read for the first time the columns of the *Star*, of social inequities and the private sufferings of Britain's working people, none of which was reported in other national presses. It was a revelation to him. He began to attend Chartist meetings, got to know Feargus O'Connor and was welcomed into the Chartist fold.

Jones saw himself as a contributor to the political cause through his literary work: 'I am pouring the tide of my songs over England, forming the tone of the mighty mind of the people.'[22]   But his contribution would not long remain so pacific.

Like Julian Harney, the written word was Ernest Jones's passion but unlike Harney, son of a Kentish seaman, Jones's father had been a cavalry officer under the Duke of Wellington before becoming equerry to Queen Victoria's uncle, the Duke of Cumberland, King of Hanover. Jones had grown up in aristocratic circles, and while Julian Harney in the 1830s, then still a teenager, was serving prison sentences at Coldbath Fields, the Borough Compter in London, and at Derby for challenging government policy on stamp duty on newspapers, Jones was receiving instruction from a private tutor before commencing his London training as a lawyer. It was thanks to Julian Harney's editorship of the *Northern Star*, in which he was beginning to insert news not just of English but also of continental organisation, that Ernest Jones set aside his future career as a lawyer for the Chartist cause. Inspired by this great change in himself he began to write poems in the spirit of a working man:

> The camp, the pulpit, and the law
>   For rich man's sons are free;
> Theirs, theirs are learning, art and arms;
>   But what remains for me?
> The coming hope, the future day,
>   When wrong to right shall bow,
> And hearts shall have the courage, man,
>   To make that future *now*. [23]

To make that political future *now*: so would Ernest Jones proceed upon his future life, to bring about a revolution in society's rule. He had lived eight years in England, 1838 to 1846, before Chartism was revealed to him, yet strangely, by 1846 everyone else felt that Chartism had run its course. There had been a great strike of all trades in 1842 when hundreds of thousands of working men, women and their children across the country had put down tools. They said they would not go back to work until the Charter was won, but too many had not been able to sustain the strike for longer than a week or two. Lancashire held out longer. This great strike had marked a crisis point for the Chartists. Hundreds were arrested by Robert Peel's Tory government. Feargus O'Connor, Julian Harney and other prominent Chartists had escaped imprisonment only on a legal technicality, and Peter McDouall escaped only by fleeing the country to France, but many less well placed were not so lucky and ended up in prison; some losing their lives behind bars or on the streets. By the time of Ernest Jones's conversion in 1846 Chartism was a side-line and Feargus O'Connor had sufficient time to argue with his editor, Julian Harney, over the direction in which the *Northern Star* was heading.

O'Connor was concerned that Harney was giving too much space to continental movements and by 1848 had lost all patience with him. '[W]hat I have so often directed should be observed,' he wrote to his editor on 4th January 1848, '...namely that, not more than one column shall be devoted to foreign news...Really the *Star* would soon become a foreign journal altogether.' Later, he qualified this with: 'You knew that...I did not include either American nor yet French nor Irish, or Italian [news] when of interest, but that I did refer to the fraternal news and conventions of all nations.'[24] By 'fraternal news and conventions of all nations,' O'Connor meant Harney's London-based Society of Fraternal Democrats, an organisation of English, French, German, Swiss, Scandinavian, Polish, Hungarian and Russian members, allied with Karl Marx's Democratic Association in Brussels.[25] The Fraternal Democrats met in a room at the White Hart behind Drury Lane, their creed: 'The principle of universal brotherhood [which] commands that labour and rewards should be equal.'[26] Harney felt it was of the greatest importance that the British radical cause should work with the socialist-democratic movements of the continent and, in spite of his employer, he continued to expand the *Northern Star* into an internationally recognised democratic newspaper. He took pleasure in ensuring that men like Friedrich Engels were given space in the *Star*'s columns. By 1848 Engels was the *Star*'s Paris correspondent.

Julian Harney and Friedrich Engels first met late in 1843, one year after the great strike. Engels was spending some time in England, having come from his home town of Barmen in Prussia to work at Manchester in the office of his father's mill. He and Harney were young: Harney twenty-six, grey-eyed, of a constitution which could render him ruddy or pale – he was vulnerable to quinsy. Engels was twenty-two, a 'tall, handsome young man, with a countenance of almost boyish youthfulness,' a 'joy-inspirer.'[27] Their first meeting was at the *Northern Star*'s offices in Leeds in the time before its transfer to London. Engels had written two articles on the continental socialist movements which Harney willingly placed in the *Star*'s columns. They became colleagues and friends. Engels had expected England to revolt during the strikes of 1842. Harney had long hoped for it but had, correctly, sensed that it could not be carried through. But both constantly saw the need, for it lived on their doorsteps.

When at leisure from his father's business at Manchester, Friedrich Engels had been going about meeting those families who, during the 1842 strike, had held out for a better life for as long as they were able. These families lived behind the offices and warehouses of the commercial district of Manchester and were effectively obscured from sight. Engels made the effort to visit them but the likelihood of others of his own class following his example was remote. None from the leisured classes was likely to venture from the main street by the south bank of the River Irk ('a narrow, coal-black, foul-smelling stream') to discover the 'filth and disgusting grime,' where twenty to thirty thousand inhabitants 'can pass into and out of the court only by passing through foul pools of stagnant urine and excrement.' 'This is the first court on the Irk above Ducie Bridge in case,' he wrote, 'anyone should care to look into it.'[28] That was Manchester. He went on to describe similar environments in other great towns of Britain.

There was enough material to go on. Engels talks of London's 'immense tangle' of streets, alleys and courts '[c]lose to the splendid houses of the rich,'[29] especially those buildings filled with families living in deep poverty in the back streets surrounding Portman Square, St George's Square, and across town on Charles Street and King and Park Streets close by Drury Lane; also of the areas dedicated to housing for the working classes in Whitechapel and Bethnal Green. He researched the events which so easily overcame the abject poor in London and they make for distressing reading –

stories of widespread suffering never really having been experienced before in so common a way except in times of war, pestilence or famine.[30] Such had been the experience of James Bezer and his mother Mary; this is how Friedrich Engels found Londoners in 1842. In February 1848 such lives manifest themselves in fifteen-year-old Eliza Pendegrass, admitted to Shoreditch workhouse in the parish of St Leonard's because she was destitute and 'has no friends.' And seven-year-old Ann Putmall admitted four days later because her destitute mother was in prison for begging.[31] These children's experiences were obscured from the rest of the vast metropolis. They happened in private and remained private. They made not a jot's difference to opinions, strategies or outcome. They did not appear in the press, not even in the *Northern Star*; they were not discussed in drawing rooms or clubs. The workhouse was there to receive Eliza Pendegrass and seven-year-old Ann Putmall when in need, but it was the system of middle and upper-class accumulation which had, according to Harney and Engels, put them in that state of need.

The joy experienced by Julian Harney and his Chartist colleagues must have been overwhelming when, after the revolution of 1848, France's Second Republic brought in a universal male franchise and workers' cooperatives. Here, they believed, were the means to a better life for the many. Joy also at the Austrian Prince Metternich's downfall and flight to England which allowed the Hungarian Lajos Kossuth to introduce a social system which required the upper classes to pay taxes, where religious choice was unrestricted and with a widened franchise. Satisfaction would have been complete when the Prussian King, Frederick William IV, was obliged to stand bareheaded as his soldiers' victims, killed during riots in Berlin, were carried before him through the palace yard. Continental states reforming, thrones toppling, political leaders fleeing to England for refuge, and a great and swift ascension of socialist-democratic bodies. In Ireland: resistance against all things English and a year-old nationalist Confederation whose members were considered too dangerous by a British government to be left at liberty. In London: demonstrations, unrest, a Chartist Convention about to assemble in order to present to parliament its demands for reform attended by a crowd of many thousands from across the country. And in every corner of Britain: families and solitary individuals unable to feed themselves. The possibility of and justification for revolution in Britain must have felt very real to Harney, Jones and McDouall at the start of 1848.

4
The Confederates

In 1848 the young attorney James Macnmara lived in very much better circumstances than London's middling and profoundly poor. His address was 9, Cleveland Row, St James, a property owned by his mother. His paternal family hailed from County Clare, Ireland, where in 1848 the famine was at its worst. How sensitive he was to this is not known. As a youth he had been the 'hope and prop of his family' until his imprisonment in 1847 at the Fleet in Southwark for debt.[32] That had been a low point and up until now there had been little improvement in his career but, after the New Year of 1848, things started looking up.

James Macnmara was the younger brother of Feargus O'Connor's friend, actress Louisa Nisbett, and in February O'Connor took James along to the Chartists' offices at 144 High Holborn.[33] A committee had been set up to look into the procurement of a London assembly hall for the express use of the National Charter Association because they now acknowledged that no agitation could succeed without London, 'the seat of government, of wealth, and of influence.'[34] The idea was that James Macnmara would act as solicitor for the committee. This was a great ascension to him; it was proper employment at last. The National Charter Association settled on the Literary & Scientific Institute at 23 John Street (now Whitfield Street) as their London assembly hall.

Meanwhile, the man who in all likelihood had introduced Julian Harney and Friedrich Engels in 1843, the Manchester Chartist James Leach, had just returned from Dublin. Leach had travelled there in January 1848 to speak for the English Chartists at the first anniversary of the founding of the Irish Confederacy. This friendly contact between the Confederates and the Chartists marked a great change from earlier years when the men who now made up the Confederacy had repelled Chartism: 'We desire no fraternisation between the Irish people and the Chartists, not on account of the bugbear of physical force, but simply because some of their five points are to us an abomination, and the whole spirit and tone of their proceedings, though well enough for England, are so essentially English that their adoption in Ireland would neither be probable nor at all desireable'.[35] The great barrier to unity of the potentially mighty force of the Irish Confederates and the Chartists was that one was nationalistic while the other was socialistic. The Confederates saw before them national freedom from English rule, the Chartists saw before them social freedom from capitalist rule. The Confederates were regarded by the British government as the greater insurrectionary danger.

Past British governments could be thankful that there had been no threat of a combined opposition to them bringing the Irish together with the English, Scottish and Welsh, but by 1848 three years of famine and coercive legislation from the Westminster parliament had changed Irish minds. The Irish Confederates were now willing to link hands with the Chartists. This was a precedent of alarming potential to the British ruling classes.

Confederate leader William Smith O'Brien was also Member of Parliament for Limerick and spent his time between London, Dublin and his constituency. By 1848 he was, if portraiture be true, a handsome, open-faced man in his mid-forties and considered by his contemporaries a gentleman. He spoke with an English accent unlike his fellow Irishman Feargus O'Connor who spoke as a man from Cork County. His colleague, Dublin newspaper proprietor Charles Gavan Duffy, describes him as possessing, 'delicacy which he pushed to weakness and a fault...but his associates knew that he would keep his word to the letter.'[36] Possessing a quiet charisma, he was perhaps not the ideal man to lead an uprising and yet it was he who would lead the attempted rising in Ireland in July 1848.

The affiliation between Chartist and Confederate had not been easily achieved. Irish Confederate Michael Doheny, friend of Feargus O'Connor, played a big part in it, also Doheny's colleague Thomas Meagher who, in May 1847, had brought a resolution to a Confederate meeting in Dublin asserting that adherence to the Chartists' universal suffrage principle was not incompatible with membership of the Irish Confederacy.[37] This was a hugely important moment and would make a great difference to what was to happen on the streets of London in 1848 as Confederate and London Chartist paraded, planned and acted together.

And the conjoining was about to happen. Three weeks after news of France's February revolution reached London, Feargus O'Connor set out from there to Manchester to meet Meagher and Doheny who had sailed from Dublin for a joint 17th March St Patrick's Day meeting at Manchester's Free Trade Hall. Repeal of the Union was the matter in hand. Expressions of fraternity between the two organisations were sturdily made in front of a huge crowd of Manchester Irish. English and Irish hands were joined at last. It was a momentous occasion. Feargus O'Connor spoke to his fellow Irish in Gaelic. In English he said that today was a sacred day and he appealed to the Chartists to help Ireland to freedom.[38] Hats were thrown into the air. These were days of heady feeling and limitless optimism for the working people of England and Ireland and their representatives.[39]

For John Russell's Whig government, especially in light of what had happened in Paris three weeks earlier, it was too much to countenance. Thomas Meagher, William Smith O'Brien and John Mitchel were arrested in Dublin four days later, 21st March, for sedition.[40]

Six weeks before this, on 9th February 1848, William Smith O'Brien had made his way from his London address at 24 Lower Belgrave Street, to the Houses of Parliament to speak in a debate on the state of Ireland.

In 1847, when the great famine was into its second and worst year, Russell's Whig government had introduced a Poor Law Act for Ireland intended to provide for the destitute and starving Irish by way of laying the responsibility entirely in Irish hands. Under the Poor Law Act, Ireland's workhouses and provisions were supposed to be paid for through subscription raised by Ireland's landlords, some of whom did their best for their tenants while many more did not. Mindful of this the Chancellor of the Exchequer, Charles Wood, told parliament: 'if the subscriptions do not come up to the full amount required...the deficiency will be made up by a rate' to be levied against the various districts of Ireland.[41]

By February 1848, everyone knew that the Irish Poor Law was not the answer. Towns where the workhouses were located were attracting thousands of disease-racked and starving people who, having made the journey there, were far too many to be taken in. At Galway it was said that '3,000 starving individuals were in the streets of that town almost destitute of clothing and clamorous for food...'[42] Earlier, George Grey, Home Secretary, had told Members of the House of Commons that the government, 'was not prepared to submit to Parliament a proposition for the resumption of...feeding all the destitute poor of Ireland by means of advances of public money.' In other words, the year-old malfunctioning Irish Poor Law must suffice, paid for by locally raised subscriptions. Furthermore, Ireland was required to reimburse English coffers for the cost of building the new workhouses required under the Act.

And so it was that on 9th February 1848, just as news of the year's first revolts across the Channel were reaching London, William Smith O'Brien made his way from his lodgings in Lower Belgrave Street to the Houses of Parliament to denounce the new Irish Poor Law Act. Feargus O'Connor, MP for Nottingham, was also in the House, and Home Secretary George Grey. Standing to make his address, Smith O'Brien said it was no solution to the failings of the Poor Law to lay the blame upon the workhouse guardians, the Poor Law Commissioners or on the landlords. 'Whoever's fault it might be, it was the duty of the Government to see that the people were not suffered to perish.'[43]

Smith O'Brien had accepted his first parliamentary seat in 1828 with the express intention of improving conditions in Ireland. His speech on the Irish Poor Laws, made twenty years later on 9th February 1848, could not have been more measured yet he must have delivered it with a heart bursting with grief and indignation knowing that many thousands of Irish were made homeless and left starving in their own land.

It was left to Feargus O'Connor, four weeks later, to more candidly upbraid his fellow parliamentarians. '[I]f the House did not legislate more justly and more humanely for Ireland than they had hitherto done, there would shortly be an end to British dominion in Ireland,' which was as much a threat as a warning.[44]   And two weeks after that, the Whig government had become, 'an exterminating Government.' He felt insulted as an Irishman 'when he saw the people starving upon a land large enough and fertile enough to maintain them all in affluence, contentment, comfort, and peace. Let the Government look to what was passing in other countries, and then say whether this was a time to trifle with the people.'[45]

These two speeches by O'Connor were made in March 1848. In his 'other countries,' namely France, the people had expelled their king, Louis Philippe, who after the February revolution fled, in disguise, from Paris, sailed to England and now was living at Claremont, Surrey. It was then that Cracow rose up, and Vienna; and here was Feargus O'Connor with a Chartist petition signed by millions of workers of Britain calling for parliamentary reform, and threatening 'an end to British dominion in Ireland,' whilst warning, in light of what was happening on the continent, against trifling with the people.

5
The Chartist Convention

The Whig government of 1848 was well aware that Irish Confederate clubs establishing themselves in London were also allying themselves with London's Chartists and that more clubs were opening. Already there was the Davis Club, meeting at the Chartist room at 83 Dean Street, Soho; the Curran Club of Westminster, which generally met at the Blue Anchor, York Street; a Somers Town Confederate Club meeting on Seymour Street, off the New Road and there were the Repealers of Marylebone.[46] And it was not in London alone. There were the Liverpool Confederates, using the George the Fourth Assembly Rooms on Hood Street, and the Birmingham Confederates who met at the Royal Oak, Litchfield Street. There were the Leeds Confederates, and the Manchester and Salford Confederates. Even on the south coast were the Southampton Confederates, meeting at the Barton Ale House on Orchard Lane. And it was not Britain alone – there was strong and active Irish nationalist support in New York. This was far more worrying to the British government than the possibility of a forcible Chartist attempt at political change. And if there were to be a rising in Ireland to coincide with a Chartist insurrection in England, the considerable military capacity available to the authorities would be stretched too far. Control would be broken.

In London in the wake of the continental revolutions and the dethronement of the French King Louis Phillipe, there were gatherings in London's East End but it was at a meeting which had nothing to do with continental revolutions that real disturbance first took place in London in 1848. MP Charles Cochrane advertised a demonstration against income tax at Trafalgar Square for 6th March 1848. Unemployment in London was high and of the thousands who turned up at Trafalgar Square on the afternoon of Monday 6th March a good number very probably were unemployed; the *Morning Post*'s reporter seemed to think so and wondered why so many unemployed would be interested in income tax issues.[47] Some left the square upon hearing that the meeting was banned by the Metropolitan Police Commissioners but many stayed, attracted by two men who appeared on the balustrade of the National Gallery with a placard proclaiming: 'The Revolution in France.'

One of these two men was G.W.M. Reynolds, novelist and recent Chartist enthusiast. After speaking against the tax on income, Reynolds then spoke for the Charter and the Paris uprising after which he left the square to the bulk of the crowd and the police.

At mid-afternoon the police began dispersal manoeuvres upon which a fight broke out between them and the crowd. Before both sides had had enough of fighting some serious injuries were sustained. Those badly hurt by truncheon blows were taken to Charing Cross Hospital. Police officers' injuries tended to be cuts from stones thrown. This was not the end of it. The crowd, by this time said to be mostly boys and young men, was enjoying itself; it tore down the hoarding around Nelson's Column and then began breaking the gas lamps in the square.

The demonstrators had numbered up to ten thousand at the start of the afternoon; by evening some one thousand remained. It was dark now. A man 'evidently mad' one eye-witness said, stood under one of the lamps to advise those who would listen to him to go to Buckingham Palace and demand the Charter and if refused to do what the Parisians had done.[48] His audience applauded him as he ran away from the oncoming police. And some did go towards Buckingham Palace, visible from the square's western side. Queen Victoria was residing there in the last stages of her sixth pregnancy. It is said some demonstrators invited the palace guards to join them as the French guards had done, then they carried on into the streets of Westminster close by Tothill Bridewell, a newly built prison which before many months would be home to a number of Chartists.[49]

The unrest, involving some looting of bakers' shops, abated in the early hours then took up again the next day.

Much to Chartist leader Feargus O'Connor's ire, G. W. M. Reynolds called a public meeting at Kennington Common for a week later, 13th March, which was followed by acts of theft in nearby Camberwell. These disturbances did not help the Chartists when the time came to present their petition to parliament for they alerted the authorities to the depth of malcontentedness in London and served to smarten police control methods.

The Home Office had good reason to prepare for trouble. It was not London alone which experienced unrest following news of the successful revolution in France. This was manifestly a national agitation and the events which took place in Glasgow on 6th and 7th March exceeded the Trafalgar Square nights of disturbance. At Glasgow there was looting of gunsmiths. Police were ordered to fire into a crowd they could not control and men were killed.

At this very time, Ernest Jones, George Julian Harney and Philip McGrath travelled to Paris where, along with Karl Marx, they met Ledru Rollin, French government minister, at the Hotel de Ville. This was a great moment to Julian Harney but he had been ill before setting out and grew worse on arrival. He finally had to keep to his bed while his friends made the journey home a few days later.

Two or three weeks after the English deputation, the Irish Confederates William Smith O'Brien and Thomas Meagher, released on bail after their arrest on 21st March, also travelled to Paris to congratulate members of Alphonse de Lamartine's Provisional Government on their success and to sound out any willingness in the new French government to allow individuals to participate in future action in Ireland. They met Feargus O'Connor's uncle, Arthur O'Connor. In both instances Smith O'Brien and Meagher came away without reassurance.

10th April, the day of the Chartist meeting on Kennington Common and great march bearing the Charter to Westminster, was getting closer.

Had there been no continental revolutions and no rioting in Trafalgar Square and at Camberwell it is likely that the British authorities would have reacted less dramatically to the imminent meeting and procession, but there was a feeling among the British ruling class that had the French king Louis Phillipe used his military unflinchingly at the time of the Paris rising he would still be on his throne.[50] They would not make the same mistake.

Instructions began to go out from George Grey's Home Office. London's magistrates set about swearing in thousands of special constables so great was the fear of the coming Chartist and Irish

Confederate march on Westminster, and the vast majority of London's propertied classes was ready to oblige in this capacity. Special constables had the authority to act against other inhabitants of London, even to kill once the Riot Act was read.

It was this English middle-class readiness to act with the authorities which differed so much from Paris's February rising. In Paris, middle-class sympathies had fallen on the side of the revolutionaries; in London that was not to be. Instead, London's middle and upper classes registered as specials in their thousands and they expected their servants and employees to follow suit. The exiled Frenchman, Louis Napoleon Bonaparte, back in London after escaping from his imprisonment at Ham and now living on King Street St James's, registered at his nearest police station. The coal-whippers at London docks were offered anything from six pence to three shillings per man by the Home Office to do the same.[51]

The Chartist Convention, which was to oversee the proceedings of 10th April, had not even met at this point. It was not until the morning of Tuesday 4th April 1848, with six days to go before the Kennington meeting and great procession to Westminster, that the delegates came together at the Literary & Scientific Institute on John Street.

Some thought they should have met sooner. John Saville, writing in 1987, stresses that the gathering of these men, following the demonstrations and unrest in London during March, 'enormously heightened public alarm.'[52] The weather during these days had turned from rain to fine, so London's roads were a little less muddy than they had been, the skies a little less grey.

George Julian Harney arrived from his home in Brompton at the appointed hour as delegate for Nottingham; Ernest Jones came from his lodgings by Portman Square to sit for Halifax; G.W.M. Reynolds was there representing Derby; Feargus O'Connor and John Shaw were the delegates for Leeds. London was represented by William Cuffay, Henry Child and James Bronterre O'Brien. Bronterre O'Brien resigned his seat within a few days. Philip McGrath was president. Chartist-Confederate Christopher Doyle was appointed secretary. The Irish Confederates were represented by Londoner Charles McCarthy. The most numerously represented districts were the northern counties, but the breadth of the delegation ranged from Devon to Aberdeen.

They settled themselves at the long table below the gallery which housed the hall's looming pipe organ where press reporters gathered, and the side galleries where an interested public watched on. Present were two government short-hand writers recording all that was said. As this first day progressed, the Convention's talk turned to the state of the country and to each region's determination to no longer leave matters to the goodwill of a parliament which ignored and derided them. In the past ten years two petitions calling for reform had been thrown-out by parliament and this third petition was to be the last. If the Charter were not won this time, then something must be done, and if that something turned out to be forceful then the towns and cities would be there to lend their weight. G.W.M. Reynolds said 'a few drops of blood were as nothing in the scale, and if moral [constitutional] means should fail, the people were prepared for any means.'[53] It was this kind of talk which induced James Bronterre O'Brien to resign his seat. He thought that the Convention, albeit representing hard-pressed regions of the country, was 'going too fast.' Of all the men sitting at that table, Bronterre O'Brien was probably the most astute political thinker and he was not a physical force revolutionary: reform must come 'gradually and justly, not by revolutionary confiscation.'[54]

For the Convention, organisation was the great issue. Without organisation and concerted effort nothing could be achieved. London had let the opportunities of 1839 go by when the South Welsh miners and foundry workers had marched into Newport and when men and women in Yorkshire had attempted a rising. London had let the opportunities of 1842 go by when the Lancashire workers had stopped all work and the strike-spirit had gripped England nearly from head-to-toe. It was critical now in 1848, with revolutions succeeding on the Continent, to bring together London and the northern counties into one great movement – a national organisation ready and able to press for change.

William Cuffay the diminutive Soho tailor, hazel-eyed, kindly and astute, told his fellow delegates that London's working classes were now, 'up to the mark. In Westminster district they increased in numbers thirty or forty per night.' London's Confederates, he said, 'were with the Chartists and would march under their own banner – the green flag of Erin, on Monday next.' William and Mary Cuffay lived close by the Davis Confederate Club which shared the Chartist's upstairs meeting room on Dean Street, Soho. They would know the Irish who attended meetings in Soho well enough. The Irish Confederate representative, Charles McCarthy, responded by saying that, 'should a single shot be fired in Ireland, forty-thousand Irishmen, in London, [are] ready to avenge their brethren.'[55]

Meanwhile, at the Home Office, George Grey increased preparations for the control of the Chartist and Confederate masses on the coming Monday. Anticipation of the event was mixed. The Duke of Wellington recommended to his acquaintances that they go about London as they normally would.[56] Others imagined a serious attack. George Grey at the very least expected vast numbers of men and women to set out from the streets of Holborn, gathering in their thousands as they made their way through the city and on, over the river at Blackfriars and down to Kennington Common to join the thousands come from across the country and then, after the meeting, for all to turn round and come back over Westminster Bridge, to the Houses of Parliament. Although the Chartist Convention was soon to give explicit assurances to the Home Office that not a window would be broken, not a stone thrown, the British government remained in a highly defensive state. It was through London's streets that tens of thousands of disaffected working people were planning to march. All the great institutions of the country were housed in the streets of the city; parliament itself was to be descended upon by this great horde of people as they came from Kennington Common to deliver their petition; the Queen was but a mile away at Buckingham Palace – the King of France had just been hurled from his throne and the mighty Metternich was now an exile while the Austrian controlled states of Italy remained in open revolt.

George Grey and the Military Secretary, Lieutenant-General Lord Fitzroy Somerset, arranged for the deployment in London of 7,122 soldiers and 1,231 pensioned military. Also available to the authorities for their defence on the 10th April were 4,113 metropolitan and city police officers and some 85,000 special constables.[57] 1,000 truncheons were sent from the carpenters' workshop at Gosport dockyard for the use of London's special constables against rioters.[58] A blow from a truncheon can kill. Risk of the take-over of public buildings by insurgents would be prevented through their occupation by troops and civilians with muskets. The British Museum, the General Post Office, the Bank of England and the Mint, the Tower of London, all were defended against the people should they rise. London's parks were to be patrolled by military personnel kitted and ready for active service. The roads around the Houses of Parliament were to be cleared of traffic and, critically, the river bridges guarded, mainly by mounted and foot police but with soldiers positioned out-of-sight and ready to act if the police were overwhelmed. The marines and sailors at Sheerness, Chatham and Woolwich were kept under arms. The electric telegraph service was taken over by the Home Office for its use only. This was preparation against an anticipated rising.

Panicking London householders sent their families from the metropolis while their servants, willing or coerced, took up the staff and wore the white armband of the special constable. Many of the coal-whippers did join the ranks of the specials, again exactly how willingly is a moot point but the promise of payment must have been nigh on irresistible. It was later said that some of the Post Office's employees had refused to sign-up and had lost their jobs because of it.[59] In these days of revolutionary possibility, the position of London's employee class was as difficult as it had been to those of the small industrial towns during the strike of 1842 when loyalties were stretched, neighbour stood against neighbour and blood for blood was sworn.[60]

As to the Chartists' preparations: nine o'clock Wednesday morning, 5th April, the Literary & Scientific Institute, and only five days from the great meeting and procession, the delegates arrayed themselves for a second day at the long table under the eye of the pressmen in the balcony and spectators crowded in the side galleries. The delegates had been sent there by their constituents with instructions to bring back the Charter but the Charter could not be brought back, that was clear to everyone round the table. All knew it would be rejected by parliament and so a plan must be agreed to carry them beyond that event. After long discussion a plan in two parts was agreed. A memorial would be presented to the Queen asking her to dissolve parliament and replace her ministerial advisors with ones who would make the People's Charter a cabinet measure, and, by way of overseeing the memorial's passage, a National Assembly was to be formed before the month's end. No man there believed for one moment that the Queen would assent to their demands but, as Ernest Jones succinctly put it, 'history must never have to say the Chartists took in blood that which they might have gained in peace.' Besides which, the memorial, 'would give time for better organisation – it would show that we were temperate,' and following the memorial's expected fate, 'the third step should show that we were brave.'[61]

On Friday, three days before the meeting and procession, came news like a thunderbolt to the Convention that the government had printed and posted up a proclamation declaring that both Chartist gathering and procession on the coming Monday were contrary to the law of the land and banned. Thirty-four-year-old G.W.M. Reynolds was despatched that morning to the Home Office to negotiate. Although his name has not survived as Charles Dickens' has, Reynolds' novels sold in greater quantities than Dickens's at this time. On Friday 7th April he made his way down to Whitehall to see the Home Secretary, George Grey. George Grey was not available and it was not until about two in the afternoon that Reynolds and his two companions, Thomas Clark and Prater Wilkinson, were shown in to see Sir Denis Le Marchant, Under-Secretary at the Home Office. The Attorney General John Jervis and Thomas J. Hall, Bow Street's chief magistrate, were in the room at the time. Reynolds gave assurance that the procession was intended only to be peaceful and that 'under all circumstances [it] would take place.'[62] Denis Le Marchant returned assurance that the government was immovable. The ban would remain.

Over Saturday and Sunday more negotiation took place between Chartists and Home Office. 'The meeting and the procession have been formally forbidden,' reported The Times on Saturday, 'and they [the Chartists] are persisting.' Persisting but ready to compromise. They offered to alter the route of the return march from Kennington Common, avoiding Westminster. The government considered. Feargus O'Connor went to the House of Commons on Saturday (he was in an invidious position being both Chartist leader and MP for Nottingham) to declare to his fellow parliamentary members that he, 'intended to attend the meeting at Kennington Common, and of coming down with the petition of the people to Westminster bridge.'[63] He did not say across Westminster bridge. Crossing the bridges was the Home Office's sticking point and he must have known it by now. Within the walls of the House of Commons he was warned by an alderman that he would be shot during Monday's procession.

Over this same weekend Queen Victoria, Prince Albert and their children left London for the Isle of Wight. A year later, Julian Harney would write to Friedrich Engels: 'well, when the Chartists were about to hold the meeting on Kennington Common to *petition* for Parliamentary Reform, the said Prince bolted...from London to the Isle of Wight and there his princeship remained until he was quite sure the naughty Chartists had gone back to their homes.'[64] On 9th April, one day before the dread event, the Prime Minister, Lord John Russell, sat down to write to Prince Albert:

Sir, – The Cabinet have had the assistance of the Duke of Wellington in framing their plans for tomorrow. Colonel Rowan [Chief Commissioner of Police] advise[s] that the procession should be formed, and allowed to come as far as the bridge they may choose to pass, and should there be stopped. He thinks this is the only way to avoid a fight. If, however, the Chartists fire and draw their swords and use their daggers, the Military are to be called out.[65]

So, the right to assemble on Kennington Common was to be respected but there would be no northward return to Westminster or to any other part of London. The tens of thousands of Chartists and Confederates, unbeknownst to them, were to be kept south of the Thames bridges and away from Westminster.

At the same time, the British parliament had the threat from Ireland to deal with. A number of British soldiers had fought each other on the streets of Dublin over the issue of repeal just two days earlier. The pressure on the British soldiery in Ireland was intense, the work they were set to do dreadful.[66] To quote one writing home to his family, their orders meant: 'turning the people out of their houses, and then we burn them down to the ground...Sometimes the people are very loath to leave their houses and little farms. You would be surprised to see the poor of this country, for they have no shoes on, and scarcely any clothing...'[67] The situation was a nightmare, and now, on the streets of London, the Irish Confederate Clubs were about to march with the many thousand Chartists to deliver their petition for parliamentary reform to the very door of the Houses of Parliament. 'The [London] Irish Confederates are as martial as their friends across the Channel,' lamented *The Times*, '...and the soft infection has spread to the English delegates.'[68]

6
Kennington Common

'A tall, dark-looking man came to visit me one day, addressing me with an air of amazing frankness: assuring me that he had been in the Detective Police force, and knew all about their system; but that he hated the government, and wanted to overthrow it and all other tyrannies upon the earth.'[69] So said Thomas Cooper, one time leader of the Leicester Chartists. In his autobiography he speaks of the volatile days of 1848 when he was approached by plotters who were, supposedly, dreaming of firing London and bringing about a Republican government. Cooper concluded that the tall, dark-looking man had been an *agent provocateur,* employed by the police force and magistrates, paid for by the Home Office. James Bezer also was befriended by one such, a man called Thomas Powell. Bezer willingly and unwittingly introduced him into the Chartist inner circle as 'Johnson'. And had he but known it, Julian Harney was taking copy for the *Northern Star* from police informer Thomas Reading, his correspondent for Irish affairs.

Ernest Jones had received a letter warning him that plain-clothed policemen were infiltrating the sittings of the Convention, conversing with delegates in a friendly manner, 'insinuating themselves into their lodgings, and then suggesting acts and deeds of an illegal kind.'[70] It was a dangerous game but one which might lead to satisfactory prosecutions and imprisonments of Chartists. More concerning even than this to the Chartist leaders who met at the Science & Literary Institute on John Street on the morning of the procession, was fear of assassination. Ernest Jones spoke of it and Feargus O'Connor had received threatening letters and now the warning in the House of Commons just two days earlier. If he were to be shot, said O'Connor, 'shooting would take place all over the country...they might shoot away.'[71] Brave words. Yet he wrote his will and last testament on Sunday 9th April, the day before the Kennington Common meeting, while seeking sanctuary in the countryside: a place where some thought he might stay. Despite the scepticism of some, there he was, at nine o'clock on that clear Monday morning, preparing to travel in one of the two open vehicles which would progress from their starting point on John Street, cross over the Thames and on down to Kennington.

It would have been a horrible moment for the organisers when, that morning at John Street, they received a note from Richard Mayne, Police Commissioner, telling them that the prohibition on the return march from Kennington across the river still stood. The Chartist Executive had hoped for a compromise on this point and the prohibition meant one of two things: defy the government, lead the crowds back across the river to Westminster and precipitate a violent confrontation between the people and the civil and military authorities, or tell thousands of Londoners and the thousands who had travelled from far and wide – Yorkshire, Lancashire, Scotland, the west country and from the eastern counties – that the main purpose of their day, the march with their petition to Westminster, was not to happen. It was Feargus O'Connor who carried the brunt of the responsibility for what would take place in the next three hours and those three hours were dreadful to him. He expected a sniper's bullet at any moment and, if he escaped that, he had to face the task of telling his 'children', as he called the rank and file Chartists, that they must turn around and go back home disappointed. Arguably, not every man at his side was mentally prepared to stand down in the face of the government's prohibition. Just the day before, Ernest Jones had told a crowd in Victoria Park: 'So help me God I will march in the first rank tomorrow, and if they [the authorities] attempt any violence upon me, they shall not be 24 hours longer in the House of Commons.'[72]

The delegates' procession left John Street just before ten o'clock that morning; the two gaily decorated vans then reined in at the Chartist Land Company offices at 144 High Holborn while the five scrolls which made up the petition (each some nine to ten feet in circumference) were man-handled into the leading van drawn by four horses. Upon the exposed front benches of the second vehicle, drawn by three pairs, were sitting Feargus O'Connor, Ernest Jones, George Julian Harney, and other National Charter Association members Philip McGrath, Thomas Wheeler and Chartist-Confederate Christopher Doyle. These men believed themselves in danger of assassination. They, with an accompanying crowd, made their way through the city's streets wet and muddy from last night's rain, along Holborn and down Farringdon Street, Ludgate Hill and on to Fleet Street, past shop-keepers and residents standing at their doors to watch them go, and on, inexorably, towards Blackfriars Bridge where a large contingent of police, some mounted, were placed, and armed soldiers under the command of Major General Brotherton positioned in four houses overlooking the river's north side. They passed over the bridge and ran the gauntlet of a body of police from L Division, drawn up in military fashion on both sides of the roadway. Once this danger was passed, they trundled on, down to Kennington via the Walworth Road.[73] Not a soldier was to be seen at Kennington but they were there, deployed early in the morning and safely out of sight.

Feargus O'Connor was fifty years old, ill, gaunt of face, short of sleep and, when he arrived at Kennington Common a little before midday and the rousing cheer of the crowd of thousands already waiting there under a clear blue sky rose up at sight of the vans carrying the petition and delegates, he was white – Richard Mayne thought white with fear. 'I never saw a man more frightened than he was,' he wrote in a dispatch to George Grey at the Home Office a few minutes after O'Connor had arrived, 'and he would I am sure have promised me anything.'[74] Feargus O'Connor had every reason to be afraid of what might happen that day. He feared assassination if insurrection were to take place. The journey to the Common was one of intense dread to him and he did say a few days later: 'it would be impossible – utterly and wholly impossible – to convey to you the faintest notion of the state of anxiety and excitement I have been in.'[75] He spent the next few weeks in a state of alcoholic intoxication but nonetheless functioned well in the House during those weeks.[76]

Kennington Common, now Kennington Park, lies some three miles down the road from Blackfriars at the junction of Clapham Road and Camberwell New Road. It was some twenty acres of 'scanty and stunted herbage', surrounded by pleasant-looking houses.[77] A vitriol manufactory stood at the Common's eastern boundary and at the south-west boundary were a workhouse and St James's Church. Just up from St James's Church, on a corner of

Kennington Road, stood The Horns Tavern. There had been heavy rain through the night. The Common's grasses were wet but the ground was still fairly firm under foot. The day had dawned clear. As soon as the Chartist delegates' procession arrived on the Common Feargus O'Connor was invited by a police officer to cross the road to meet Police Commissioner Richard Mayne at The Horns Tavern. The crowd thought this was an arrest but Mayne only sought the opportunity to impress again upon O'Connor that no procession would be allowed to re-cross the Thames' bridges back north. The immense dangers and appalling consequences of any attempt to lead the great crowd across the river to Westminster after the meeting were made clear.

Later, Ernest Jones was to say that it was men who would not act 'because it is forbid,' who were to blame for that day's humiliation, but on this Monday morning, 10th April 1848, the die was cast; yet still the great crowds – many there perhaps thinking that this time the Charter would be gained – had no idea that they were to be denied their long anticipated procession to Westminster.[78] On the Common these thousands were assembled under their various trades; a great many banners and their insignia marking each out. The Irish Confederates had marched there eight abreast. A young tailor by the name of Robert Crowe was one of their number and he paraded with the rest at the Common's south-eastern side. And milling around the assembled trades and Confederates were hundreds of unaffiliated demonstrators and onlookers. William Cuffay was there as a Chartist delegate. James Bezer, George Mullins, Joseph Richie and their friends were surely there although there is no direct record to say so. Police Commissioner Richard Mayne was told that a few men were carrying pikes 'with handles about 6 feet long', and he was alerted to the presence of foreigners in the crowd.[79] Any French presence would be thought sinister and it is said a shadowy man, a Confederate Francophile named Churchill, had travelled from Paris to assist at this time and was on the Common that morning.[80] Mayne observed that the foreigners were taking no active part. Estimates of the crowd's number vary wildly. David Goodway, writing in

1982, thinks it not unreasonable to estimate some 150,000 people gathered on the Common's twenty acres at the meeting's peak.[81]

While Feargus O'Connor stood upon one of the vehicles to address those nearest to him, Julian Harney and G.W.M. Reynolds went off to address the gathered Irish Confederates. Ernest Jones stayed by O'Connor. By now, each man knew what he must do. The crowd had been excited by O'Connor's meeting with the Police Commissioner and he had difficulty quietening them.[82] He began to speak: 'My children...you were industriously told that I would not be amongst you today: well, I am here!' There came a roar of welcome.[83] He had received death threats but would choose a dagger to his heart before giving up Chartism. 'You all know that for a quarter of a century I have been mixed up with this democratic agitation; in Ireland since the year '22, in England since the year '33, and as you know I have never shrunk from taking my share of all the responsibility...let me now implore you...let me enjoin – nay, I would go down on my knees to beseech you – do not now destroy the cause I have so struggled for all my life.' He was cheered, and when he asked all who were 'prudent, sensible men' to raise their hands, a forest of hands was raised.

'The authorities have not, though they threatened us, interfered with this meeting on Kennington Common...We, at least have had our meeting. The government have taken possession of all the bridges...the [Chartist] Executive have decided that you shall not be brought into collision with an armed force.' By now the situation would be dawning on those near enough to hear him: 'I come now to disperse you. You will not walk in procession. You must go peacefully to your homes.'[84]

There would have been a sinking in every heart at Feargus O'Connor's words. Some reports say that once he had left the Common (which he very soon did to go straight to the Home Office to assure George Grey that peace had been maintained) dissatisfaction rose up. William Cuffay urged the march upon Westminster as planned but no procession formed. The shock and disappointment must have been dreadful. The organisation had been immense. Thousands had travelled for many hours over many miles to be there this day to march upon Westminster. As if in tune with the mood, the clear blue sky above began to cloud over. At a quarter to one there were more people leaving the meeting than joining it. Mayne wrote: 'O'Connor has just left in a cab. Meeting seems broken up.'[85] To where could all these thousands of people go now that their procession was not to take place? One of the Confederates, Robert Crowe, says that for nearly three hours everyone was held as prisoners south of the river.[86] Many who had travelled from the northern counties had met at Hyde Park before making their way to Kennington, they and everyone else who lived on the north side had to go back across one or other of the bridges but the bridges were closed, defended by police on foot and on horseback and with soldiers waiting in reserve.

All that morning the police contingents entrusted that day with guarding the bridges would have been steeling themselves for the first sight of the demonstrators returning up the road from Kennington. This was the flash point, and they, the men of the police force, were the first line against any revolutionary attempt. Were they, like John Russell, expecting knives and swords? The crowds, despite having heard that the way was closed to them, did make their way there because they must – it was their way home. When the moment came, the bridges' defenders responded forcefully. At Westminster Bridge, leading directly to the Houses of Parliament, the police dispersed the oncomers with their truncheons. One elderly man was knocked down and carried away, presumably by friends, leaving his hat behind on the roadway.[87] At Blackfriars Bridge, to where Richard Mayne went from the Common, the police drew themselves up in three divisions on the southern side, while another division and mounted officers cleared the street from the bridge down to Stamford Street. The demonstrators who first arrived at Blackfriars Bridge were trapped between the police horses and their comrades coming up Waterloo Road. 'I think not more than 14 or 15,000 persons,' Mayne despatched. 'Mr Malalieu believes there are nearly 20,000.'[88] Truncheons were used here too, and the great crowd was driven down Holland Street and Stamford Street.[89] The effect upon the people who came to Kennington Common this day is barely imaginable and afterwards Chartism began its decline.

In the interim, the ten horses which had drawn the cars carrying the petition and the delegates that morning had been safely led off to a stable, and the great petition, which was to have been carried triumphantly to the doors of parliament, was abandoned, left to lie alone in its van which now stood on a deserted Kennington Common. Three cabbies arrived on the Common at mid-afternoon, collected the rolls and took them off to the House of Commons while the two empty vans, their flags presumably still attached, were drawn away to a near-by livery. It began to rain, heavily.

The opinion of historians of Chartism is that there was no plan for revolution on 10th April 1848. The Kennington Common demonstration was intended to pressurize the government into agreeing to the terms of the Charter. But the middle and upper classes of London feared that revolution was intended and the possibility of it most surely crossed the minds of some of the delegates and demonstrators. One of O'Connor's close friends, Thomas Allsop, had written only four days earlier to Robert Owen, then in Paris: 'any attempt to stop short will be suicidal...the revolution must be accomplished...private property must be shared....'[90] Bronterre O'Brien resigned his seat at the Convention the day before the procession and his biographer, Alfred Plummer, thinks it likely that he knew more about the intentions of the London Irish than he revealed.[91] As it turns out, the working people of London and the visitors from the rest of the country were profoundly and very ably humiliated by the ruling classes of London on 10th April 1848. 'The misguided mechanics who were called from their homes for this precious 'demonstration' may be pitied; the men who called them, must be despised,' said one of London's daily papers the following morning.[92]

Although the theatres and many shops were closed on 10th April 1848, parliamentary business went on as usual and also that of the Central Criminal Court where eleven men were sentenced to seven years' transportation for petty thievery and other misdemeanours committed at the time of earlier mass meetings in London.

By the late-afternoon of the 10th, people were beginning to make their way freely over the bridges to the city side of the Thames and the crisis was considered, by the Duke of Wellington, to have been dealt with. However, the next day Lord Palmerston, Foreign Secretary, wrote to Ireland's Lord Lieutenant, Lord Clarendon: 'Things passed off beautifully here yesterday, but the Snake is scotched not killed, we must continue on our guard.'[93] His assurances would bring small comfort to the Lord Lieutenant at Dublin Castle, for things there were very difficult. 'A great social revolution is now going on in Ireland,' he had recently advised the British prime minster, 'the accumulated evils of misgovernment and mismanagement are now coming to a crisis.'[94]

As to the Chartist leadership, a tipping point had been reached in the minds of men like George Julian Harney, Ernest Jones, Peter McDouall. And so began elections for delegates to the Chartist National Assembly to take over from the Convention. The Assembly's stated purpose: to send a memorial to the Queen asking for her indulgence. Its practical purpose: to organise for action.

7
Prelude to the June Crisis

While telling the demonstrators on Kennington Common that they must go home, Feargus O'Connor audaciously brought to their attention another matter. The Treason Felony Bill was to have its first reading in the House of Commons that very day. This Bill, if passed, would make any person expressing opposition to the Crown or Parliament guilty of felony, by which they could be transported for fourteen years or for life. With the passing of the Treason Felony Act, 'you [will] be armed with the effectual means of sending Messrs. Mitchel, Meagher and Smith O'Brien to Botany Bay,' wrote Lord Campbell to Lord John Russell, which shows to what lengths the Whig government was prepared to go to control the uncontrollable Irish.[95]   Feargus O'Connor called upon the Kennington Common crowds to petition parliament against the Bill. An answering voice instantly expressed the general feeling: 'No more petitions!' If petitions, constitutional means, were no longer to be employed, then what? And indeed, there would be no more Chartist petitions, the time for that was over.

After a long absence, William Smith O'Brien entered the Houses of Parliament on that very afternoon of 10th April at much the same time as the People's Petition arrived there from Kennington Common. O'Brien had returned to speak against the Treason Felony Bill (otherwise the Crown and Government Security Bill). While being ridiculed and laughed at while speaking, sometimes to the point of uproar, he assured the House that their attempt to coerce Ireland into submission by such means was futile and he warned, were they not to yield to Ireland's claims for a separate legislature, that Ireland would seek to become a republic. Did England really want a French republic to her east and an Irish republic to her west? [96]

George Grey, alluding to Smith O'Brien's recent visit to Paris, accused him of seeking foreign aid to subvert the British government and played with the word traitor. Feargus O'Connor, his ghastly day echoing in his words, made some protestation against the Bill then George Thompson for Tower Hamlets warned against a hasty decision on approving legislation which made 'the speaking of words on political questions a felony.'

The Treason Felony Bill passed into law with impressive speed. It received its third and last reading in the House of Lords on the 20th April, ten days after its introduction. Queen Victoria put her signature to it two days later. It remains active to this day.[97]

After three days in the hands of a House of Commons Committee, the great People's Petition of 1848, claiming to be endorsed by some five million people and having undergone seventeen hours examination, was declared to contain not above 1,900,000 signatures. This seemed to nullify it in some way. Feargus O'Connor had 'pretty strong collateral proof,' he told the House on 13th April, 'that the number of signatures to the petition had far exceeded what the Committee had reported.' Lord John Russell gave all credit to the Committee, adding that, 'they could not take into account the great number of idle people and passers-by who, seeing a petition at the corner of the street, might have thought fit to sign it, without having any wish for the Charter.'[98] Joseph Cripps, Conservative member for Cirencester, followed this up with his own defence of the Committee's findings. He had taken a look at the petition and calculated that for every 100,000 signatures 8,200 were women's, which seemed to nullify it still further. Cripps then went on say that O'Connor had lied about the petition's weight which O'Connor promptly challenged. O'Connor was as promptly challenged by the Speaker. Mr Cripps said: 'if any Member of the House had laid himself open to the charges which ought to deprive him of every credence to which man is entitled,' that man was Feargus O'Connor. The embattled O'Connor defended himself again then, presumably at his wits' end, walked out of the Chamber.

Thus the Great People's Petition of 1848 was first left to lie alone in a van on Kennington Common, was rained on as it was taken to the Houses of Parliament, was said to contain some 1,900,000 signatures not the five million claimed, eight percent of which were mere women's and others purporting to be 'Queen Victoria' 'Duke of Wellington' 'Pugnose' and other false titles, to contain 'language the most disgusting...which the vilest strumpet in the street would blush to name,' and thus ridiculed was finally rejected as swiftly as the Treason Felony Bill was passed.[99]

And at this very time, in Paris, things were playing out in remarkably similar fashion for Louis Blanc's socialists. On 16th April, three days after the fate of the Chartist petition was settled at Westminster, the French socialists marched on Lamartine's Provisional Government sitting at the Hôtel de Ville, and demanded, 'the abolition of the capitalist system and the organisation of all work on a co-operative basis.' The Provisional Government dispersed the socialists with a newly-formed 'garde mobile' – the Lamartine government seems to have learned a lesson from the English example set six days earlier on the 10th. In parallel with the Chartists in London, the socialists of Paris went away to reassess their situation. This was the beginning of the end of those great hopes of imminent reform held by Ernest Jones, Peter McDouall, Julian Harney and so many others, although they perhaps did not acknowledge it to themselves just yet. The Chartist National Assembly was about to convene in London – an Assembly which it is reasonable to say considered itself an alternative people's government.

Julian Harney was not at the Scientific & Literary Institute on John Street on 1st May 1848 when the Chartist National Assembly, called by the dissolved Convention of April, gathered for the first time. At least he was not there as a delegate. His employer, Feargus O'Connor had warned that if he were to insist on being part of a National Assembly then he could do so only by resigning his editorship of *The Northern Star*. The same choice was given to Ernest Jones, also employed by the *Star*. Ernest Jones pressed on with the National Assembly. Julian Harney chose to keep his job but within twelve months would be describing O'Connor as, 'a thorough aristocrat masquerading in the outward profession of democracy...But I believe the hour of his fall is at hand,' which it was.[100] O'Connor's professional and private life began to unwind in tragic fashion through business failure and syphilitic neurosis so that, within four years of the events described here, he had descended from being the charismatic leader of a national movement into a patient at a Chiswick asylum. After 1848 the Chartist organisation went forward with diminishing input from O'Connor.

On that first day of the National Assembly, observers were admitted up to the galleries and balcony of the Scientific & Literary Institute by a young family man named John Fussell who normally spent his time employed at a jeweller's shop in Clerkenwell. Once everyone was settled the delegates presented their credentials. Those for London's districts were Alexander Sharp and John Shaw for Tower Hamlets;[101] William John Vernon and Henry Child for West London; James Bassett and Thomas Martin Wheeler for South London; two Confederate members, Charles McCarthy and the mysterious Churchill for the city and Finsbury, but McCarthy soon withdrew. Francis Looney, a cabinet maker by trade, spoke for the London Confederates but, despite the recent closeness of the two organisations, the Confederate body at Dublin would only go so far as to wish the Chartist National Assembly success in their aims, they would send no representatives. The Irish lawyer and nationalist John Mitchel had been selected for Rochdale but had written to say he could not attend. Peter McDouall represented Nottingham. Feargus O'Connor, who represented Nottingham at Westminster, was of course not there. According to O'Connor, the National Assembly 'did not represent the Chartist party,' and was 'the origin of every act of persecution' to which the Chartist movement was subsequently subjected.[102]

Poignantly, on this very day an Act of Parliament, long fought for, came into effect. This was the Ten Hours Act, inspired eighteen years earlier by Huddersfield's Richard Oastler. It was intended to bring a degree of social control to an uncontrolled industrial system which was largely responsible for the suffering which would be discussed this day at the Scientific & Literary Institute. The Act's great accomplishment was to reduce women's and their children's working hours in textile mills to ten a day, eight on Saturdays. Working people of the northern counties had long agitated for it and from that campaign of the 1830s, together with the Anti-Poor Law campaign, the great mass of people who made up the Chartist movement had coalesced in 1838. Ten years on, and here was that same Chartist body reshaping itself in a hall behind Tottenham

Court Road at the very moment of the Act's implementation. As it turns out, middle class industrial entrepreneurs soon found ways around the restrictions imposed upon them by the Ten Hours Act, and herein lay the great issue: should the Chartists join forces with those members of the middle-class entrepreneurs who also wanted to see political reform? Could the middle classes ever be trusted? It was an issue the Assembly touched upon and one which Chartists would consider and internally battle over for years to come.

On the second day of the Assembly's sitting Ernest Jones, Halifax's delegate, explained to his companions how disillusioned by petitions, how impatient of memorials his constituents were, and that they were ultimately willing to break what he termed 'political' laws. He said a National Guard had been formed at Aberdeen ready to support the National Assembly and the same support existed at Dundee, Edinburgh, Paisley and Glasgow where there was great suffering. Mr Hoyle of Salford said starvation there made the people impatient. The underlying message was that the country would respond if matters came to a head in London.[103]

On Monday 8th May, Peter McDouall urged upon the Assembly a strategy he had been proposing for years: that the country should be divided up into districts for the purposes of sound and practical organisation.[104] 'Each district to be divided up in localities, each locality into wards, each ward into sections. Each ward to consist of 100 men, each section of ten members...the district officers to keep an active superintendence over the localities, and to furnish weekly a report to the Executive, stating the number of members, as also the state of trade, the general feeling of the people, and the movements of all public bodies.' Ernest Jones urged that 'every man supply himself with arms in the exercise of his constitutional right.'[105] And a request to present the promised memorial to the Queen was made to George Grey. This request would soon be blocked by Grey's Home Office.

Meanwhile, William Smith O'Brien, whose appearance on 10th April at Westminster's Houses of Parliament would be his last for his trial for sedition was nearly upon him, returned to Ireland and on 22nd April he arrived at Limerick. As soon as people heard that he was there some hundreds gathered outside the Confederate Club's premises on William Street expecting to hear him. Smith O'Brien was reluctant to appear. He was tired from his journey and would rather have stayed in his room but was persuaded to address the crowd; in fact he was left little choice when a musical band played right up to the door of the house where he was staying. So out he came and made his way to William Street where the cheers for him were deafening. He spoke from a first-floor window while below a tar barrel burned to give light to the night, illuminating a large tricolour flag, orange, green and white, which 'floated from one of the windows.' 'I am glad,' he said, 'to find that I have not suffered in your opinion by a state prosecution...the British government may learn that the spirit of the Irish people is not to be subdued by prosecutions or coercion acts...' [106] The orange, green and white flag received especial comment: 'I hail it as a happy omen that you have thus united those emblems which formerly were the insignia of faction in this country, the orange and the green. Henceforth that flag will be the Irish tricolour as a sign that the Protestants of the north and the Catholics of the south will unite in demanding the rights of their country.' Smith O'Brien begged them to sustain this principle. From the start, the Irish Confederation had been religiously non-partisan. Smith O'Brien and John Mitchel were Protestants, Thomas Meagher and John Dillon were Catholics, and so it went on among Confederate numbers. The Catholics and Protestants must unite in the cause of national freedom.

On Saturday 13th May, three weeks after Smith O'Brien's speech at Limerick, John Mitchel was placed in Dublin's Newgate prison to await his trial for felony, and two days after that, on the morning of May 15th, William Smith O'Brien, having returned to Dublin to face his own trial, was escorted from his lodgings on Westland Row by hundreds from the Confederate Clubs of the city. When this great procession passed the steps of Newgate prison on Green Street, John Mitchel's wife, Jane, was seen leaving from there and was given a great cheer. She acknowledged with a wave of her hand. Once arrived at Dublin's Court of the Queen's Bench the Clubs' members dispersed, leaving Smith O'Brien to face a jury from whose list all but three Catholics had been struck. It was reckoned that there was a good deal of Catholic sympathy for the

Confederate cause and a sympathetic jury was not what the British government wanted. Despite this attempt at what was described by some in the press as jury packing, Smith O'Brien was, surprising to all, found not guilty through the refusal of one Catholic juror to agree to his guilt. The same happened at Thomas Meagher's trial the next day, although the number of Catholics on his jury was now reduced to one. Smith O'Brien and Meagher found themselves free men. This had not been the British government's expectation and this was not to be the fate of John Mitchel.

John Mitchel's trial came up ten days later. As far as the British authorities were concerned, a man as popular and revolutionary as Mitchel must be put away. His trial ran from the 25th to 27th May 1848. He was found guilty under the Treason Felony Act. The charge of jury packing was now a heated issue. In London on the 29th, William Keogh, MP for Athlone, stood up in the House of Commons and asked Lord John Russell: 'Is it a fact that on the late trial of Mr. John Mitchel for felony, every Roman Catholic was excluded in open court by the Attorney General, without any cause assigned?' The prime minster responded by reading out a letter from Mr Monahan, Ireland's Attorney General, explaining that: no, the men had not been struck from the jurors' list because of their religion, it was because of their politics. This seemed to make everything all right:

> [When] a party is to be tried for a political offence...you should set aside on the part of the Crown, without regard to their religious opinions, all persons whom...you find to entertain political opinions according with those of the prisoner and the associations by whom he is supported. I am clearly of opinion that to leave such persons on the jury would be to defeat the administration of the law, and be totally inconsistent with the true principle of trial by jury, which is, that the juror should be indifferent between the Crown and the prisoner.[107]

Upon which Henry Grattan, member for Meath, got to his feet. 'Does the noble Lord,' he asked the prime minister, 'say that every Roman Catholic professing repeal principles is to be excluded from juries?'

The prime minister replied, 'I think the words of Mr. Monahan are very right and judicious, and I have no hesitation in adopting them.'

No matter the claims and counter claims in the House of Commons of jury packing, on the streets of London things were not so ambiguous. Even during Mitchel's trial, meetings had been taking place in London and now what was about to happen was in reality as dangerous to law and order as the Kennington Common meeting had been perceived to be.

8
June Crisis 1848

Peter McDouall and Ernest Jones believed their plan of organisation for Britain was 'capable of affording our movement an irresistible power...the government dread our organisation more than any other measure.'[108]

That organisation encompassed the nationwide districts, localities, wards and sections proposed by Peter McDouall. And the London based Chartist Assembly itself was organised into an Executive Committee of five, with a Financial Officer, and twenty Commissioners ready to step into the shoes of any Executive member who might find himself otherwise occupied as a state prisoner. An element in the National Charter Association had emerged which saw the risings in the capital cities of the Continent as examples to emulate. The voice which had called out 'No more petitions' on Kennington Common six weeks earlier spoke for the many who had lost hope in constitutional means. In a sense, the realisation of just how hopeless it all was seems to have freed the minds of many Chartists from the thrall of men whom they were beginning to think cowards; and the word coward began to be used often towards any who would not stand their ground, who were not willing to break the bounds. A Combined Chartist and Confederate organisation was attempting to raise itself to meet the smooth and well-armed machinery of an experienced establishment.

Since 1829 London's police force had been formed into seventeen districts covering an area from Peckham in the south to Hampstead in the north, West Ham in the east to Hammersmith in the west. Police Commissioner Richard Mayne had defined the new force's purpose as the protection of life and property, the preservation of public tranquillity and the absence of crime. At first, the new police had not been liked. It was considered intrusive and what is more had to be paid for through taxation which touched everyone, but by the time of the events of 1848, now with national police forces in play, many of the middle and upper classes thought it money well spent; the declared objectives for which the police had been organised were demonstrably attained. A critical aspect which everyone, aristocrat, industrialist, shop-keeper and operative, understood was the force's utility as an instrument of social control.[109]

Yet, almost always, beneath the buttoned blue coat of the Metropolitan police officer was a man who came from the same kind of family as those he was expected to keep down. They, who made up the front line against London's insurgent crowds, were seen by those crowds as the tool of the establishment. 'We are styled "bludgeon men", "government minions"' said one Metropolitan policeman. 'Permit me to say there are as good men in the police force as out of it.'[110] But these were days of class war in Britain and, as one Chartist concisely put it, 'it was the labouring class that made the tyrants so strong, by being such fools as to enlist and fight their battles.'[111] It was a mighty and well-oiled edifice, that of the establishment. Landed aristocrat and industrial entrepreneur deployed soldier and policeman while the churches deployed moral power sometimes like a weapon. There was little hope of agitators breaking through this. It would need the middle classes, like those of Italy, Prussia, Austria and France, to oppose the ruling elite before so much as a dent could be made upon establishment defences, but the British middle classes, happy enough to contemplate the landed aristocracy's diminution, were solidly with them when it came to insurgency. 1848 would not play out in Britain as it had on the Continent. The agitators might organise all they chose, the Home Office had spies and informers to infiltrate the most secret of meetings, and *agents provocateur* who would lead dissenters on into waters from which they could not rise; and the Home Office had the middle classes at its back.

On the evening of Monday 29th May 1848, the day after news reached London that John Mitchel was found guilty and would be transported for fourteen years under the month-old Treason Felony Act, thousands of Londoners began to gather in the city. Already Mitchel was aboard the war steamer *The Scourge* which would take him to the penal colony of Bermuda and his conviction and transportation was to produce disruption in England of a momentous kind. On Stepney Green in London's Mile End some three thousand came together and, in the light of an early spring evening, listened as Ernest Jones railed against the packing of Mitchel's jury. Then they heard Peter McDouall praise the men and women of Bradford who, the day before, had stood up to the police and finally had been controlled only by the military.[112]

In the same hour, to the west of Stepney on Clerkenwell Green, John Fussell stood on a van with Joseph Williams, baker by trade, and the Irish Confederate Charles McCarthy, to address another large crowd gathered there. Behind them sat some others including two freelance newspaper reporters, Henry Potter and Frederick Fowler. Fowler reported Charles McCarthy to have said that now was the time 'to strike the blow. Ireland may, for aught I know, at the present time be in arms; but if she is not, she is only remaining quiet in order to recruit her strength the more effectually to strike the blow, and release herself from tyranny and oppression.' Then John Fussell is said by Potter to have uttered the fateful words: 'What made the Emperor of Austria fly from his country? Why, the fear of assassination; and it is by these means that other bad rulers will soon fly.' For this, Fussell would be accused of inciting assassination and imprisoned for it. To his brother, he denied having said it. Two witness at his trial backed him up.[113]

Meanwhile, the Stepney Green contingent formed themselves four or five abreast and, setting out, were led upon their way by Joseph Williams and William John Vernon down the Whitechapel Road.[114] They were part of a great march to parade westward through London. 'A set of grim, dirty and discontented men,' is how *The Times* describes them. Howsoever they might appear to some, they went, in marching order, up Commercial Street, Sun Street to Finsbury Square. There they waited for some time until those from Clerkenwell Green joined them. Keeping in file, this now massive crowd made its way up Chiswell Street towards Smithfield Market, then down Snow Hill, up Holborn Hill and along King Street. It was growing dark and, as they went, local residents stood in groups watching: 'The Chartists are out,' one was heard to say. Now away from the city's confines and getting dangerously close to the streets leading to Westminster and the Houses of Parliament, this great file of people crossed the Seven Dials and Leicester Square then worked its way up to Dean Street in Soho where, as they passed No. 83

where the Chartists and Confederate Davis Club met, cheers were raised, then onwards they went to Oxford Street as if to go away from the West End; but no, they turned down Regent's Street, back towards Westminster. This was a massive procession of marchers which, according to one eye-witness, was rising to 80,000 or 90,000 bodies.[115] They had come out for John Mitchel, but more than that it was something to make up for the banning of their march to Westminster on 10th April, it was something to show that they had the power to do such a thing if they chose, it was something to show their numbers and their organisation. It has an aura of the mysterious about it, this grand, bold and declaratory march through the streets of London on 29th May 1848.

From Piccadilly they made their way to Trafalgar Square. It was now about ten-thirty at night. The square was lit by gas lamps. Now that the great body of marchers had reached the streets and squares so close to Westminster forbidden them seven weeks earlier, they found that a force of police, bearing not just staves but cutlasses, was waiting. St James's church yard was filled with specials on stand-by, St James's park gates were closed and across the park the Duke of Wellington's residence standing at the south-east corner of Hyde Park was defended by police. The military, it is said, 'were all under arms.'[116] After a while the head of the massive procession set off again, not towards Whitehall and the House of Commons but away, eastward, back to the city via the Strand, and as it went the crowd grew thinner as people made for their homes. It is almost as though the demonstrators and the authorities were performing some kind of ritual the rules of which were understood by both. The night did not end altogether peacefully. Some one thousand remained on Red Cross Street outside John Cartwright's Coffee House which was a Confederate Club and Chartist meeting place and where, according to police officer Horace Hardy of G Division, Joseph Williams told everyone from an open window to meet 'night after night until such time as they had news from Ireland...when our Irish brethren will want us to assist them in obtaining their liberties.' But the crowd wanted action 'Tonight! tonight!' They were promised more action for the next night and William John Vernon, at the window with Joseph Williams and

Charles McCarthy, is said to have advised them to bring guns and pistols. [117] This volatile remainder, some of who by now had been drinking, clashed with police close to midnight. To the eyes and ears of some, this might have looked and sounded much like the preliminaries to a rising. Those participating seem to have felt it so.

In the hours following the great march through London, Police Commissioner Charles Rowan was told by one of his undercover informers, George Davis, that the leaders of the vast march 'had hard work to keep them from firing the houses – the mob wished to take possession of the houses of parliament. The Confederates and Chartists seem to have the greatest confidence in their power and a day is named, tho' known at present to but a few, when they will rise armed en masse, and they think no power the government can bring will be able to resist them.' Davis, who acted as a leading member of the Chartist Wat Tyler Brigade at Greenwich and reportedly expended much energy in selling weapons to his Chartist and Confederates colleagues, also mentioned the man Churchill. [118] Such was the threat Police Commissioners Charles Rowan and Richard Mayne were to live with through the summer months of 1848.

The Houses of Parliament were not attacked on the night of 29th May but over the following six days, Tuesday 30th May to Sunday 4th June, something looking very like the opening phase of revolution took place in London, and the sentencing of John Mitchel was its trigger; the action, then, being largely within the purview of the Confederate Clubs. The Chartists roundly declared support for their Irish brethren; they regarded Mitchel as a 'patriot, and his persecutors as the real traitors.' [119] This is what happened as reported. The day after the great march of the 29th, the Metropolitan Police banned all public processions. A meeting took place that very evening on Clerkenwell Green attended by prominent Chartists Joseph Williams, Alexander Sharp and the Confederate Thomas Daly, so the next day, Wednesday May 31st, the police banned all meetings. [120]

That evening a crowd estimated at four thousand men and boys again gathered on Clerkenwell Green, in the pouring rain, in open defiance of the prohibition. Although there had been an official

Chartist presence the night before, there seems to have been no leading Chartist or Confederate present on this third night of demonstration, only one man called Dunkard showed leadership by climbing a lamp post and from there urged the crowd that now was the time to agitate and to be determined.[121]

A large contingent of police, two troops of the Horse Guards and the local magistrates, ready to read the Riot Act, were before the crowds. There were, though, soldiers concealed inside Clerkenwell church, more police and military pensioners waiting in readiness within the Session House, and special constables had been placed in the houses surrounding the Green. Calls for Mitchel and the Charter were heard from the crowd. At about nine o'clock the police began to clear the area while some of the demonstrators called out 'stick together' but police truncheons are weapons hard to withstand. Even so, the number of people so increased as the evening went on that many streets around Clerkenwell were thronged by thousands; there were clashes between demonstrators and police on Saffron Hill. Some tried to raise crowds farther east in Finsbury Square where the whole of the Honourable Artillery Company had taken up quarters across the road on the Artillery Ground. This was a prolonged confrontation of huge proportions taking place in the streets of London yet a police force greatly outnumbered and exhausted from three days of active duty was able to keep control of the city's streets that night; their organisation outstripped anything their leaderless foes could muster.[122] The point at which insurrectionary action gains its own momentum was not reached, perhaps because there was no real leadership to direct it.

The civil authorities could deal effectively with undisciplined crowds who found it difficult to coalesce in the vastness of London but the two things so greatly feared were an armed populace and fire-raising. The main gas pipes at Farringdon Street were vulnerable according to the informer Davis and this alarmed the authorities because their disablement would plunge the city into darkness.[123] Militant organisation with the capability to disable London in this fashion was something to fear. Until then, Chartist organisation had come in on the coat-tails of the action of others: the miners and iron foundry workers of South Wales in the November of 1839, the trades' strike of August 1842. Now it was organising on its own account together with London's Confederate Clubs. And it was not London alone which was raising riot. Bradford, Halifax, Huddersfield, Keighley, Otley, Bingley, Leeds, Manchester were out too. This was a widely coordinated insurrectionary effort.

Londoners were again on Clerkenwell Green the next evening, Thursday 1st June, doubtless anticipating a continuation of the previous night but critically still no leading London Confederate or Chartist presence was apparent. One anonymous person dressed in a brown holland blouse did make a fiery address from the pavement opposite Clerkenwell churchyard with the clear intention of urging more decisive action than that of the night before. He was of sufficient prominence for the crowd to give him their attention. He called them cowards because they had not resisted the police the previous night. 'We did,' came the reply. 'You suffered them to knock down your friends in the same manner the horses are slaughtered in Sharpes-alley, you are not fit to be called Chartist or Repealers.' The crowd is said to have groaned at this harangue but were urged by the speaker to go to work. They could pull up the pavements before the police arrived. Where, he wondered, were their broken bottles and old mantle-pieces which John Mitchel had recommended as ready weapons? [124] When the police did arrive, a little after eight o'clock, the speaker had left the Green and the crowd was armed with stones and sticks but aimless in its purpose. Nonetheless, it took two hours for the police to clear the Green and its surrounding streets. M division under Superintendent Evans was left to keep guard.

Clerkenwell Green saw yet another gathering on the Friday night although it seems to have been a desultory affair compared with the previous two nights. Again, it is said that no leading Chartist or Confederate was there to direct.[125] There is strong suggestion that the Chartist leadership was over-stretched and possibly overwhelmed by the extent of activity showing itself in the streets, despite their having urged it. The situation in the northern districts of the country was one of riotous demonstration yet no revolution coalesced, no advantage was taken of the situation. The climax came forty-eight hours later, on Sunday, 4th June, when two official mass meetings were held by the Chartist Association and the Confederate Robert Emmett Club at London's Bishop Bonner's Fields. Now a small number of Chartist leaders were ready with encouragement but, if a rising was in their minds, their encouragement came too late.

Bishop Bonner's Field lies on the west side of Victoria Park in Bethnal Green. Victoria Park had been open to the public for about two years and Bonner's Fields had for many years been given over to gravel and clay pits; before that it had formed the parkland of the Bishop of London's palace. But even before anyone assembled on Bishop Bonner's Field on Sunday 4th June, serious morning clashes took place between demonstrators and police.

The night before, Superintendent Johnson of Islington's N Division had learned of a 'monster' meeting to be held on London Fields, Hackney, and so ordered his men to be on the field at 5 am. There, in the growing light, he saw 'a Rank of Men distance from me about 6 or 700 yards, when I saw them I fancied they were probably at Pike Exercise. I accordingly formed my men in line at extended order in the rear, and charged upon them, when within 100 yards of them they ran away in all directions.'[126] So there were drill exercises going on that morning and a little later a preparatory speech was made to a crowd of some five hundred in the neighbourhood of Virginia Fields in Bethnal Green, to which Superintendent Johnson's men were again called. Here the speaker urged everyone to 'show the vile police, if they came there, that they were not afraid of them.' They scattered, nonetheless, as soon as the officers of N Division appeared, but then regrouped.

By now church-goers were at their services close-by, gathered in little oases of peace as police endeavoured to disperse the demonstrators with 'indiscriminate' truncheon blows in the streets around them.[127] Stones were thrown. Some police were injured. Many more demonstrators were injured. The fighting went on for more than two hours. At the same time, in Victoria Park itself, a similar number was scattered by mounted police who hit out at them with the flat of their swords. And this was just the preliminaries to the meetings called by the Confederates and Chartists for that afternoon and evening.

At around three o'clock on the Sunday afternoon of 4th June the Confederates opened their meeting on Bonner's Field. There were angry speeches against the conviction and transportation of John Mitchel. The police did not interfere although occasional cries of 'the police are coming' were made. The Chartists followed at five but the crowd was left waiting for the speeches to begin as the men to give them had not turned up; it seems the Chartist leadership was experiencing a crisis of some sort at this point. Alexander Sharp was the only speaker there and said that those absenting themselves were cowards in the face of danger from the police but that he did not care 'one pin for the police or the military.'[128] He applauded his listeners for their action that morning but upbraided those who kept running away from police attacks: 'when you have about three to one, one man falls out of three, and the other two can secure him. Now, will any man tell me I am wrong when I say that you acted the part of cowards when you ran away?' At last Ernest Jones appeared on the field. Jones, a good speaker with a strong voice, stood on a chair to address the crowd:

'All that I say is this, stand fast by your colours...and if you see any bodies of police coming near to this meeting, marching on to this meeting, stand your ground, shoulder by shoulder. Do not run...Dare them to strike you...it is your own cowardice that invites others to strike a blow. It is men saying, 'We will not do this, and we will not do that, because it is forbid.' Make up your mind, – stand by it, – and, whatever comes, stand your ground...There is no use coming among you when there is no organisation, and it is not the executive that can get up the organisation. Show us your organisation, and we will show you how to get your rights...Only organise and you will yet see the green [Chartist] flag floating over Downing-street. Let that be accomplished, and John Mitchel shall be brought back again to his own country, and Sir G. Grey and Lord J. Russell shall be sent out to exchange places with him.'[129]

All this while a man called Matthew Robertson, resident of Bonners Hall, was watching proceedings from his front window some 150 yards from the speakers. At about seven-thirty, soon after Ernest Jones had left Bonner's Field, Robertson realized 'from the rapid movements of the populace that something unpleasant had occurred and I saw the Police with their truncheons endeavouring to disperse the Crowd.'[130] It is said to have started with a large group throwing stones at St James Church which stands close by the field and where thirty-six policemen from K Division were concealed. Howsoever it was, a great many from the crowd began running away from the oncoming police towards Victoria Park's Lodge gate which was promptly closed by the park's superintendent, Samuel Curtis, for fear of the damage so many in a panic might cause. He fell in the rush.[131] Events this day, however, were going to play out differently from other days. With Alexander Sharp's and Ernest Jones's words still ringing in their ears, a good number of the crowd stood their ground as the police came at them. According to a newspaper not Chartist friendly, the police used their truncheons 'with full force, without the least regard to persons...many had their heads broken [and] arms fractured.'[132] The thirty-six policemen who had been waiting out-of-sight in St James Church under the supervision of Inspector Waller came out onto the field and a larger body of police, some mounted, some from Islington's hard-pressed N Division, quickly joined them. The crowd inflicted injuries as well as receiving them. St James's incumbent, Henry Philip Horton, is reported to have seen men with 'stones, sticks or clubs and one at least with an Iron Bar,' but he was sure of stones and sticks only when giving evidence at Alexander Sharp's subsequent trial.[133] One man's knife-thrust at a policeman's torso was deflected by his victim's hand. Some others were hurt by blows.

This is descriptive of a London crowd engaging with the police in unusually determined fashion. A great many of the Bonner's Field crowd of 4th June 1848 did stand their ground, having been encouraged by their leaders, against those they reckoned to be the tools of their oppressors. As evidence of the challenging and prolonged nature of this battle between populace and police, the fighting carried over onto nearby streets, first along Bonner Street running down to Green Street, and then over a much wider area. This was the point at which Metropolitan Police members collectively reached the end of their tether. They ran amok through the streets of Bethnal Green, going into private houses, making attacks upon public houses and beating innocent bystanders.[134] The man Dunkard, he who had climbed the lamp post on Clerkenwell Green two nights before to address the crowd, was badly injured during this battle. He was seen a little later that evening covered with blood which flowed from a sabre cut to his head while he made his way to G.W.R. Reynold's Wellington Street premises. Dunkard, impassioned and keenly offended, was arrested and taken to Bow Street police station where his wound was dressed.[135] His fate from thereon is not known.

Of all the events which took place in London in 1848, the days from Monday 29th May to Sunday 4th June were the most likely for revolt but there seems to have been no-one of sufficient leadership to grasp the moment. The battle on 4th June was a very serious business, but at the time the Chartist leaders' focus was on eight days hence, 12th June, a day on which they planned to stage a show of such strength to the country that the government, and the civil and the military authorities would no longer be left in any doubt of it. So, the days of greatest promise to the agitators, those final days of May and early June when matters had gone beyond a mere show of strength, had passed them by. At the Bonner's Field Chartist meeting of 4th June, Alexander Sharp said that the leaders had absented themselves for fear of the police; Ernest Jones was the one Chartist Executive member to attend the meeting and he soon left the field. After his speech he went directly to Euston Railway Station to board the mail train to the northern counties to prepare for the demonstrations scheduled there for the 12th. He left London at a crucial time even though perfectly aware that 'the whole of the country is now looking to London.'[136] He left behind the people he had urged to stand against the authorities, and a Home Office now ready to instruct the police to arrest him. A warrant was made out against him by the Bow Street magistrates two days later.

'On what authority,' George Grey the Home Secretary was asked in the House of Commons by Tower Hamlet's MP George

Thompson on the morning after the Bonner's Field battle of 4th June, had the police 'by violence, unprovoked...undertaken the dispersions of the crowd at Bonner's Field?' The answer came: 'They were acting under instructions directly given to the commissioners of police by [my]self.' Grey went on to assure the House 'that the most effectual measures would be taken by the Government to prevent the recurrence of these tumultuous assemblages.'[137]

Two days later Thompson, now armed with sixty complaints from witnesses living in his constituency of Tower Hamlets of unprovoked 'outrages' which were 'perpetrated by the police, not merely in Bishop Bonner's Fields, but more than a mile from the spot where the Chartist meeting took place,' again put the same question to George Grey. Grey started his reply with a brief concession to local complaints then said, 'I have heard as yet nothing whatever – which in my opinion can detract from the praise which is justly due to the police.' He believed the Chartist and Confederate meetings over the past few days to have been 'intolerable nuisances to the loyal and well-disposed in the localities in which they were held,' and he had received many letters attesting to it.[138] Thereafter the matter was dropped and the House moved on to resume a debate on the Navigation Laws. But George Grey would not leave matters entirely in the hands of the police for the next Chartist demonstration: the great demonstration planned for 12th June. The magnitude of the danger just passed would be appreciated by all. For 12th June, soldiers would be deployed as they had been for 10th April.

The outcome of the 4th June 1848 infraction in Bethnal Green and across Tower Hamlets brought a realization to some in the Chartist leadership that their organisation must be stepped-up. On the evening of the 4th the Confederates and Chartists of the Bermondsey district decided upon the appointment of twelve men able to properly coordinate joint action to 'carry out a vigorous agitation' for the Charter and repeal of the Union.[139] A similar meeting was held by the Wallace Brigade at Strutton Ground, Westminster. The *Northern Star* prepared to reprinted, for its front page, details of the plan of organisation adopted back in May. Most significantly, the first of a series of secret meetings of a group which would evolve into a conspiratorial Ulterior Committee took place two days later, on Tuesday 6th June, at the Windsor Castle, Holborn. This secret committee met four times in June: twice at the Windsor Castle on the 6th and 13th; once on Monday 12th at the Albion beer shop on the Bethnal Green Road, and a fourth time on 14th June at the Chartist assembly hall itself, the Scientific & Literary Institute on John Street.[140] By their second meeting the planning for an insurrection was in hand. Amongst those who were leaders of this group were Peter McDouall, George Mullins, James Bassett and William Lacey. There were at least fourteen in this early grouping, one being George Davis the government spy. The initial members would be joined in later weeks by others including James Bezer, William Cuffay, and a second government spy Thomas Powell who would give all the evidence needed by the authorities to send the rest to prison. Ernest Jones might very likely have been a member of the Ulterior Committee had not his imminent arrest made that impossible.

PART TWO
THE SUMMER RISINGS

9
The June Plot

Upon quitting Bonner's Field on 4th June, Jane and Ernest Jones travelled to Manchester. Having spent the night of the 6th at Manchester's Moseley Arms Hotel, they were awakened early the next morning by Inspector Haynes of the Metropolitan Police Force who carried a warrant for Jones's arrest. Jones had expected to attend another of those great open-air Chartist meetings at Blackstone Edge a few days hence but that was not to be. Also arrested early that morning at their London homes were Alexander Sharp, John Fussell and Joseph Williams. Ernest Jones was immediately brought back to London on the morning train from Manchester and met his arrested colleagues at the bar of Bow Street police court that same day. Here they were charged with sedition. The next day, 8th June, William John Vernon was arrested for 'inflammatory' speechmaking and for taking part in the extraordinary night-time procession of 29th May. He was committed for trial on these counts. Bail offered for Ernest Jones by Feargus O'Connor was rejected and the sums apportioned to the others were far beyond anyone's means to secure. The British government was removing from the field of action the men most likely to cause trouble. The prisoners were kept at London's Newgate prison until their trials.[141] This sudden move against the Chartists in advance of their country-wide demonstrations planned for the Whit Monday holiday of 12th June rings of the authorities' final determination to sweep away the Chartist threat.

Apart from Ernest Jones, the Chartist Executive was still intact and at liberty. Its four remaining members, Peter McDouall, James Leach, Samuel Kydd and John McCrae, were now thrown into a dire situation with so many of their close colleagues suddenly swept up by the authorities. Until now, the government had made no mass arrests and this dramatic departure must have thrown a new and startling light on the Executive's planning for the coordinated demonstrations to be held on Monday 12th June 1848. Their stated purpose was to demonstrate just how strongly the people wanted the Charter. Their justification for this demonstration was that its constitutional alternative, presenting a memorial to the Queen, was lost because the government had placed a barrier between them and the Crown. Now the government had made a decisive and aggressive move against them. The Chartist Executive's letter of 10th June to the 'Wardens of the Chartist Body' of London asked them to assemble their numbers on the 12th and advised: 'We expect it will be a peaceable demonstration but, at all events, be prepared for the worst. We leave it to your own discretion to come up in what manner you please, knowing you to be sensible men – and we expect every man to do his duty.'[142] This was not a directive of clarity from the Executive. Its recipients were left to read between the lines.

The next day a crowd at Iron Wharf Paddington was dispersed by police and a man was charged with drawing a knife and threatening to stab police officers.[143]

And so again, unease within the ruling parties due to Chartist activity grew intense. The Attorney General, John Jervis, later admitted that a general uprising was anticipated 'throughout the whole kingdom.'[144] In response to London's planned Chartist meeting of Monday 12th June the ban on all public meetings was reasserted through the Commissioners of Police, although it was anticipated that the demonstrators would ignore it. The propertied classes of London had exulted at the authorities' resounding success in April at the time of the Kennington Common meeting but here they were again, confronted by a Chartist threat with quite a different face to it. Hundreds of gun barrels as well as cases of guns, muskets and rifles, were known to have been sent by Birmingham's manufacturers to London during May and were still being sent in June. Inventories of arms dispatched were sent to the Home Office by Birmingham police inspector Charles Field and, by way of illustration of the threat, the Home Office received a letter from a mechanic called Palmer, employed on government works, saying he had overheard a workmate's description of a recent Chartist meeting attended by a great many men with pistols and other weapons. The weapons were 'needed for Whit Monday' – 12th June.[145]

The pressures upon Charles Rowan and his front-line police force to keep control of such a threat were patently very great; he wanted matters settled once and for all. Rather than prevent the 12th

June meeting from happening, Rowan favoured allowing the people to gather for this would give him and the government ministers to whom he answered the opportunity to disperse the insurgents at the time of their choosing, and decisively: it must be decisive, otherwise their opponents 'would occupy the houses with such firearms as they may be provided with, and if so it might be necessary to call in Troops.' Downing Street would not want to call in troops. Troops against populace signalled loss of governmental legitimacy and this they wanted to avoid. Rowan's plan, which he noted in a memorandum of 10th June, was much more likely to bring matters to 'a final settlement...taking it for granted that the law is clear as to the dispersion.'[146]

It seems that the bloody fight between the Chartists, Confederates and police which had not materialised on 10th April but which had escalated, controversially, into a running battle on 4th June, was now considered a necessary evil to be faced, gone through and won. Rowan called his superintendents together at Great Scotland Yard the next day to give his final instructions.

Civil and military defensive arrangements for 12th June 1848, almost as great as those of 10th April, were prepared against the demonstrators by the authorities: three troops of the Royal Horse Artillery; twelve squadrons of cavalry, one of which was to be placed out-of-sight on the south-eastern boundary of Bonner's Field; ten corps of infantry; four hundred military pensioners also placed out-of-sight at Bethnal Green workhouse at the western tip of the park. On stand-by out of town were 144 of the 12th Lancers and 544 Coldstream Guards. In other words, 304 officers; 5,399 rank and file, 910 horses, 3 Howitzers and 3 light 6-pounders.[147] Troops were placed at Millbank Penitentiary, the City Bridewell, City Compter and Newgate to defend against assisted breakouts. All this was undercover: the frontline force against the Chartists would be a large police presence waiting for them on Bonner's Field, the massive military presence to back them up being kept well out-of-sight.

Considering the government ban, and considering the civil authorities' duty to uphold that ban by all means necessary, 12th June gave the perfect opportunity to the Chartist leadership to demonstrate its determination to stand its ground, 'shoulder by shoulder,' should those means be employed. David Goodway, writing in 1982, thinks that by now the Chartist leadership, 'would probably have welcomed the Bonner's Field demonstration developing into a rising.'[148] There was an atmosphere of dreadful anticipation attaching to this event. Whit Monday celebrations were taking place across the country and Chartist Executive members Samuel Kydd and John McCrae went out of London to attend those of the eastern and western counties, James Leach was in Dublin, so it was left to Peter McDouall to remain in London to oversee the meeting at Bonner's Field. He arrived on the ground at about one o'clock on Monday 12th after having learned that the police and military had taken over the area. Getting down from his cab and walking onto the field he saw how extensive the police presence was. A large force was positioned along the field's perimeters. But it was not a field taken by police alone which met his eyes. 'A vast concourse of persons, including a great number of women and children were attracted to this bivouac,' reported one of his companions.[149] Sellers had set up stalls. Families had come out, it being Whit Monday and a holiday, all presumably unaware of the large military presence no distance from them.

'I went amongst the police,' said McDouall, 'and demanded of several inspectors an interview with the magistrates.'[150] He was directed to Bethnal Green's workhouse close by, where the four hundred military pensioners and their commanding officer were quietly positioned, along with the local magistrate Mr Arnold. Mr Arnold, according to McDouall, warned that the government would not allow the meeting to take place and that 'if it does, I must do my duty.' Arnold's duty, as magistrate, was to broadcast the Riot Act after which unlimited action against civilians was allowable; an action for which Police Commissioner Charles Rowan was fully prepared and which he intended as a means to a final settlement of the matter.

Peter McDouall decided to retreat. 'I will not risk a murderous collision with the immense force collected here.' The Chartist Executive had had a great deal to assimilate in the week running up to this day: the running battles between demonstrators and police and subsequent arrests of prominent Chartist figures. Matters had reached a critical point. Peter McDouall had probably anticipated the immense force he encountered that afternoon, certain it is that he had already been talking of ulterior action with colleagues as he now, having called the meeting off, straightaway went to join the cabal (the secret or Ulterior Committee) which had first convened the previous Tuesday, the 6th. This, then, is the moment when Peter McDouall abandoned what faith he retained in open and legitimate demonstration.

That afternoon's rain which was to send everyone in London's East End for shelter might well have started to fall as McDouall made his way to the Albion Beer Shop on Bethnal Green Road where the Ulterior Committee was meeting. It was not far from Bonner's Field. Whatever these men at the Albion Beer Shop had expected of that afternoon's mass meeting, they now embarked on an organised plan of insurrection while the rain shower turned into a great thunder storm which passed over their heads. There were twenty-five delegates present; two were police informers. One informer was George Davis, second-hand book and furniture seller, the other Thomas Reading. Reading was no less than the *Northern Star*'s correspondent for Irish affairs and had been betraying his colleagues for nine years, so he was a sophisticate when it came to the practice of espionage.[151] The secret committee had, or felt itself to have, control over Chartist and Confederate movements and the power to make authoritative decisions. This is borne out by what Thomas Reading told Police Commissioner Richard Mayne of that upstairs meeting. All out-door meetings were to stop (this would bring an end to fruitless demonstrations and has the ring of Peter McDouall's clarity of thinking).

'The whole of the Chartists and Confederates to meet in their various localities every evening for the next ten days and not to leave their Clubs without being desired to do so by a messenger sent from the delegate council.

The meetings of the delegate council to be permanent and secret, the place of meeting not to be made known...The object of the council is also to [be] kept secret from all Chartists and

Confederates...The government to be taken by surprise at midnight, and to be done within ten days from this time.'[152]

Reading also claimed to have seen bludgeons, pistols and knives in the Albion Beer Shop's parlour below. 'I have not the least hesitation in stating that anarchy was carried on to a great extent this day.' Reading then advised Mayne that he would be at the statue at the Whitehall Gardens the next morning (Tuesday) at half-past-ten 'to see Mr Yardley should you wish to communicate anything to me.'

And so, practical planning for a rising scheduled for the third week of June 1848 was now in hand. The Ulterior Committee met again the next day, 13th June, at the Windsor Castle public house, then Peter McDouall, James Bassett, William Lacey, George Mullins and four others including the spy George Davis, were bold enough to meet on the following morning, Wednesday 14th June, not in the relative obscurity of a public house, but at the Chartist Assembly Hall, the Literary & Scientific Institute on John Street, to discuss how best to go about the rising. A map of London was spread out, maybe upon the great table around which the delegates of the National Charter Association and the National Assembly had talked in earlier weeks, and over this map a system of barricades was discussed. The area they could secure by barricading would stretch from the Strand north-eastwardly to Clerkenwell, then down to the Barbican and back again. They were looking at a large area, rich in pawnbrokers' and gunsmiths' shops where there were arms. And there was the possibility, they saw, of extending the barricaded area over the river to the Kent Road in Southwark where the police station there could be taken.

At close of this daytime meeting they agreed to gather again that evening at The Lord Denham on Great Suffolk Street, Southwark: the coordination of London with other towns ready to rise was yet to be arranged. Then soon after, something panicked Peter McDouall. It is said that John McCrae received information which prompted McDouall to send an urgent message to the delegates at Southwark waiting at the Lord Denham to tell them they were dissolved 'by the order of the Executive.'[153] The man charged with taking this message asked him for clarification: was the plan off?

McDouall said something to the effect of what plan? On hearing this, the Southwark conspirators felt themselves betrayed. Exactly what happened to cause this sudden and complete close-down remains unknown. Did McDouall and McCrae realise that there were spies among them, feeding everything they planned through the police to the Home Office? The spy Davis attended sensitive Ulterior Committee Meetings for weeks after this day, so clearly not him. Had Reading been found out? Had Feargus O'Connor intervened? No-one knows.

In all events it is apparent that it was quite simply an impossibility for the conspirators to keep their plans secret. A letter which found its way to the Home Office the next day, 15th June, is proof again of this. William Jordan, a workman living at 64 Nelson Street, Blackfriars who, even though a self-declared victim of their system and evidently not in their pay, gave warning to the Home Office of the plot because he could not bear to see London 'suffer the horror of a general conflagration.' The plan of incendiarism was too much for him. 'I make the following communication which may be relied on,' he wrote. 'On Wednesday eve next after wages time, it has been decided to hold moveable street meetings...every man not carrying fire arms to carry a link [torch], and lucifers, which he is instructed to use as circumstances may suggest – but the grand object is not only to accomplish a revolution which they do not expect, but to set fire to entire streets, which they deem practical. Their object is to produce universal consternation and alarm.'[154] And so the Home Office was well alerted to Chartist and Confederate intentions through letters of this kind without even having to rely on paid informers. Whatever the actual cause, the June plot was abandoned. There were to be no barricades, no burnings, no rising, so that London continued along its way; the Home Office quietly went about its business, and the Chartists and Confederates went about theirs.

June ended peacefully in London but in Paris it did not. There had already been great shock when the result of the first election based on a universal male franchise returned a government overwhelmingly dominated by the propertied middle classes. In Paris twenty-four Socialists had stood as candidates, three were elected. Now, in June, what happened in Paris demonstrated to everyone the likely outcome of a London rising. On 21st June the workers' greatly prized cooperative workshop scheme was closed down by Lamartine's government. This produced consequences of a dreadful kind. Over two days the working people rebuilt their barricades, at the Porte St. Denis, the Faubourg St. Martin, and the Faubourg St. Antoine. But this time, unlike February, the National Guard stood with the military against the barricaders. In the four days between 23rd June and the 26th, at least ten thousand socialist insurgents were killed or wounded; they took with them a great many soldiers and the peaceable Archbishop of Paris, killed at one of the barricades. If Peter McDouall and his colleagues had built their barricades in London as planned, the entire middle and upper classes of London, backed by an overstretched and out-of-temper police force soon to be armed with serrated swords on loan from the Tower Ordnance, together with a military growing increasingly difficult to restrain, would have met them likewise.[155] Whoever averted that event averted a piece of British history of unknowable consequences.

The authorities chose not to arrest Peter McDouall for another four weeks and the leading Confederate, Thomas Daly, who was implicated in the June plot, managed to get himself to Paris within a few days. Chartist Executive members Samuel Kydd and John McCrae kept themselves at reasonable arm's length from the Ulterior Committee's activities which allowed them to continue in their official Chartist positions. John McCrae did, though, stand by his fellow Chartist Executive member McDouall in the days following and both men continued to speak out in public.

10
The Irish Rising

Feargus O'Connor, still the nationally recognised leader of Chartism, albeit a disjointed movement by this time, had no faith in revolutions, believing them to be made by those who become the oppressors. Although he was a man decried during his life time by a great many as an unprincipled adventurer, O'Connor was more principled and scrupulous, and more incisive than those who despised him were willing to acknowledge. He might not have liked revolution but he understood the utility of the threat, and this he had maintained for years. However, the threat was now showing every sign of becoming a reality and he made it known that he was not so keen on that. By late July 1848 the likelihood of an attempted revolution in Ireland was raised to a certainty. How this might affect things in a Britain of such volatility was a critical question.

After John Mitchel's transportation in May, the Irish Confederates in Dublin had formed a new Council led by William Smith O'Brien. Among the nineteen Council members were Terence Bellew McManus, Thomas Francis Meagher, Michael Doheny and John Dillon.[156] These men would stand by Smith O'Brien through the entire campaign to come. Also, James Stephens and John O'Mahony, neither of who were of the Council, would figure large in the events rushing towards them. The Confederate Council's openly declared purpose was:

'...the overthrow of the power of the British legislation in this island. That while we are firmly resolved to abstain, in our political capacity, from any interference in matters of a religious or sectarian character, we are not the less desirous that religion should be upheld, and the legitimate influence of its ministers maintained in its integrity. That so far from desiring to overthrow social order, and to subject our country to universal anarchy, our first anxiety has been, and is, to secure the legislative independence of our country with the least possible injury to any class of its inhabitants; and in the accomplishment of these our designs we hope to put an end for ever to the sufferings and the disorders which have never ceased to afflict our people under the sway of Britain.'[157]

In London, this Confederate declaration was read out to parliament by Lord John Russell on 22nd July 1848. Three days later parliament suspended the Act of Habeas Corpus in Ireland. All protection against immediate arrest for stating opposition to English rule in Ireland was taken away. This came as a profound shock to the Confederates and propelled them into untimely action. It was a case of flight or fight for them. O'Brien would not flee so, there and then, they prepared to fight. Thomas Meagher assured him everyone was prepared to take the field with him.[158]

It was a time of bleak portent, but at least potatoes had been growing wherever they could be stuck into the ground, and everyone looked forward to a good harvest. All looked fair until the very week of the suspension of Habeas Corpus when Dr John Lindley of the Scientific Commission wrote from Ireland to tell Trevelyan (now Sir Charles Trevelyan and still in charge at the Treasury) that the blight was back and widespread. It showed itself with ghastly swiftness and certainty in mounds of rotting, stinking potatoes. '[W]e are in the hands of Providence,' Trevelyan wrote, while the prime minister, Lord John Russell said he was 'lost in despair.'[159] And now even the weather turned to wet. Confederate hopes of a rural population fortified and ready for action after a good autumn harvest were dashed, there being no potatoes to fortify anyone. But at least funds were on offer. According to Charles Gavan Duffy, two agents from New York had arrived at Dublin and were seeking contact.[160]

And so the Irish rebellion of 1848 was on. The Confederates' tried to muster the clubs at Kilkenny for the opening of the rebellion, then, realising the military presence there was too great for them, they decided on Carrick farther to the west in Tipperary. While the suspension of the Act of Habeas Corpus was passing through parliament these matters had already been settled so that, by Monday 24th July, William Smith O'Brien and his colleagues had reached Carrick. They were met there by John O'Mahony, a thirty-two-year-old local land owner, who it is said, 'threw himself from his saddle and, tossing the bridle on his arm,' hurried to join them.[161] O'Mahony came with the news that the country between Carrick and

Clonmel was 'ready to take the field.' He urged them to raise the revolution that very night, starting with Carrick after which it was reckoned the insurrection would rapidly spread. Duffy recalls seeing a 'torrent of human beings, rushing through lanes and narrow streets...eyes red with rage and desperation...' He could feel too, that, '[i]t was the revolution, if we had accepted it.'[162] But they did not accept it; they did not grasp the moment. The substantial and ready force which John O'Mahony brought that day to Carrick was allowed to disperse. O'Mahony went back to his house; his thoughts and feelings can only be vaguely imagined, for in that moment all chance of a successful rising was lost. '[T]hat subtle electric force whose influence evades arithmetic – vanished away,' wrote Duffy sometime later.[163]

There was something in William Smith O'Brien which was not suited to the revolutionary he was supposed to be. His revolution was a necessity not an ambition and it would be honourable. No illegal confiscation or damage of property, nothing taken that was not paid for. His tall figure was dressed in military fashion for the occasion, clad in black, a plaid scarf tied across his shoulder, but his expression according to Club leader Charles Kickham who met him the next day in the road at Mullinahone was of 'a man in a dream.'[164] 'Don't go like a rabble,' O'Brien had said. 'Put your Club into order.' With them stood John Dillon who, glancing first at the twenty-year-old Kickham then at the little crowd which made up the Club, had responded to this with 'something peculiar' in his smile. Smith O'Brien was loved and honoured by his compatriots; he inspired an unwavering loyalty. He was not, though, a man by any degree sufficiently brutal to lead a rebellion.

So, they went to Mullinhone where they unfurled the green flag. They went to Ballingarry where John O'Mahony rejoined them. They sought support and appealed to the miners of Slieveardagh Hills. The local priests came out to tell the people that they were 'rushing on ruin.' Smith O'Brien is said to have sat down on a bank 'while silent tears of shame and despair ran down his cheeks.'[165] On Friday 28th July, he and John Dillon wearing a blue military cloak thrown across his shoulders, were rejoined by Michael Doheny,

Terence Bellew McManus, Thomas Francis Meagher and others, all of who had been busy raising support elsewhere.

In London on Thursday 27th July, mention of possible trouble in Ireland appeared in small sections on the inner pages of the *Daily News* and *Morning Chronicle*. *The Times* printed a two-column report on the eighth page of its issue. Later that day in parliament, and at about the time that William Smith O'Brien was said to be despairing on a Tipperary bank side, the MP for Limerick, William Monsell, had picked up on obscure rumours of an uprising in Ireland and asked George Grey to inform the House. George Grey had 'great satisfaction in stating that he had every reason to believe that the alarming accounts which appeared in the late editions of the morning papers...of an insurrection having actually broken out in the south of Ireland, were totally destitute of foundation.'[166] In the meantime, Grey's Home Office arranged for pre-emptive action against any possibility of organised sympathy-risings in England, Scotland or in Wales through arrests of Chartists and Confederates. Peter McDouall had already been arrested ten days earlier, at Ashton-under-Lyne.

Two days before MP William Monsell's quizzing of the Home Secretary in the House of Commons, a large gathering of London Confederates had met at the City Theatre on Milton Street, close by Moorgate. The building and street outside were thronged. At that meeting no-one mentioned the rising in Ireland, the London Confederates did not know of it, but Metropolitan Police G division, M division and L division were ready to suppress any disturbance just in case any did, and plain-clothed officers from F division were deployed among the meeting's members.[167] The next afternoon, London's Lord Mayor, James Duke, watched police exercises on the Artillery Ground, just up the road from the Milton Street theatre, and 'expressed himself highly delighted with their military movements.' A few hours after that, James Bezer made his way to the City Theatre to speak at another radical meeting, this time of Chartists. Again, there was no mention of the Irish rising.[168]

Then, two days later, on Friday 28th July, Bezer attended yet another meeting at the City Theatre and this time people knew that something was afoot in Ireland. Bills had been printed advertising:

"Is Ireland up?" About one thousand people were there, many women, many Irish labourers, 'such a class of people as is usually seen at chartist [*sic*] meetings.'[169] James Bezer read out loud to the theatre crowd extracts from the *New York Herald* printed in a June copy of the London *Times* expressing the view that 'England stands upon the brink of a fearful revolution...such a revolution is as much wanted as it is inevitable.'[170] He would not, though, have read out the *Herald*'s opinion of working class Londoners which was ungenerous: '*they are a degraded race, hanging loose upon society, destitute of moral force and principle, who, when they move, move only to rob and to plunder, to break windows, and, at the sight of a few policemen, to run away.*' Or might he? Bezer, a man of lively humour, probably agreed to some extent with this; he had, after all, lived in the most degraded streets of London all his life and knew their varied character well. He did, though, make good use of the *Herald*'s inevitable revolution against the British government's misrule, and added for himself that 'neither a roguish government nor an insane government ought to exist.' Bold talk as rumour of revolution in Ireland was reaching England.

The Chartist and Irish Confederate networks of London were a few hours ahead of the general public because even now only an intimation of the rising in Ireland was filtering through via the London presses. The *Liverpool Times* ran a heading, 'Outbreak of the Rebellion' in its late edition of Friday 28th July. In fact, the rebellion had been in effect for four days and the Confederates were about to have their conclusive stand-off with the police at Boulagh Commons, two miles north of Ballingarry.

On Saturday 29th July, forty-five police officers from Callan, under the command of Captain Trant, retreated before Smith O'Brien's force of men and women to a nearby farmhouse on an elevated piece of land. The farmhouse was owned by Margaret McCormac whose husband had died of famine fever the year before. As chance would have it, Margaret McCormac was away from home when the police took it up as a place of defence against the rebels but her five young children were inside the house and were kept there. When she returned, the distraught mother sought out Smith O'Brien and asked him to parlay with the police. Together they went up to the farmhouse parlour window where O'Brien shook hands with his adversaries and asked them to surrender. Captain Trant was given time to consider this offer (time in which reinforcements would arrive) and he kept the children. Reports state that Smith O'Brien and his supporters were fired at when, in frustration, some threw stones at the farm house and that in the following exchange of shooting O'Brien rather than falling back with the rest 'became desperately determined, and stood in the midst of the fire without any purpose.'[171] It is as if O'Brien knew this moment to be the apogee of his service to Ireland; it is as if he were willing to die for his cause that day. James Stephens and McManus went to pull him to safety and were injured. Stephens ended up hidden in a ditch. Two were killed in this exchange of fire, a young man called Thomas Walsh, and Patrick McBride a stone breaker whose wife tried to reach him as he lay dying. Of the injured, John Kavanagh received a bullet in his thigh and another severely injured man, James Dwyer, went into hiding in the Slieveardagh Hills.[172] The end came when police reinforcements from Cashel arrived and fired into the remaining group of rebels at the crossroads to where they had retreated.[173]

On the same day, Saturday 29th July, the London papers carried full reports on the Irish rebellion; at the day's close the Confederates were fugitives – but not William Smith O'Brien. He refused to hide. 'I won't be a fugitive where my forefathers reigned.'[174] Nor did he want to endanger those who might give him shelter so, even though a bounty of £500 was on his head, he went openly upon his way to Cahirmoyle, his home in Limerick, to his wife Lucy, five sons and two daughters. But he never reached them. He was caught while boarding a train at Thurles.[175] Arrests were made in Dublin, and the Confederate Clubs there and elsewhere closed down. Across Ireland many Confederate members involved in the Boulagh Commons attack managed to evade arrest as they headed for coastal spots in their attempts to leave the country. There are tales of disguises. John Blake Dillon, dressed as a priest, managed to board a brig in Galway Bay; he eventually made it to New York. Three others sailed from the Shannon to Constantinople while Michael Doheny and James Stephens were to spend weeks moving from hiding place to hiding place in Ireland. And then there were the many who were less well known and not written about in later years: James Dwyer, the man so badly injured in the farmhouse battle, was at last found by police on Tuesday 15th August, hiding in one of the Ballingarry colliery pits. He was taken to Clonmel gaol. So the rebellion had failed. But not everyone felt it was over. John O'Mahony, still at liberty on his Carrick estate, was one not ready to give up.

Upon receiving the simultaneous news of the O'Brien led rising and its failure, London's Confederate Davis Club met in the upstairs Chartist room at 83 Dean Street, Soho, on 31st July. Despite the ambiguous news, the excitement was now unrestrained. The Irish tailor, Robert Crowe, came from his home in Camden Town to attend the meeting and gave full voice to his excitement. He knew plain-clothed policemen were in the room and he did not care 'for those persons present who wear other people's clothes. I do not care if what I say is criminal. I, for my part, shall do all in my power during the next week to put a stop to trade, and urge the Irishmen in London to rebellion.'[176] Brave talk, for Robert Crowe was inviting the law to pick him up and put him away, which is exactly what it did.

11
August Conspiracy

'The law has triumphed, and we obey the law.' So said the two remaining Chartist Executives, Samuel Kydd and John McCrae in the *Northern Star* in July 1848.[177] The law did, indeed, deal most smoothly with anyone who challenged establishment bodies. The Attorney General, John Jervis, had made a lucid argument for the prosecution at Ernest Jones's trial on 10th July at the Central Criminal Court and now Jones, together with Alexander Sharp, John Fussell and Joseph Williams, was imprisoned in Tothill Fields Bridewell and would stay there for the next two years. Francis Looney, leader of the Confederate Davis Club on Dean Street, had been tried two days earlier, on 8th July, for using seditious language. He was found guilty and sentenced to two years' imprisonment. It was something of a conveyor-belt exercise for the government. The lawyer James Macnmara had assisted at Jones's trial at the Old Bailey and was still spending hour upon hour at Bow Street station as men were taken there. The Chartist Victim Fund was not large and a solicitor's fees are not small. Legal costs started to mount.

'But who made the law?' Kydd and McCrae put to their *Northern Star* readers: 'The Whigs nominated the Attorney-General...the Attorney General is, in name and law, the representative of the Crown, but in office and act [is] the prosecutor on behalf of a corrupt and despotic faction of her Majesty's subjects.'[178] The events of June and July 1848 exactly demonstrate why Chartism had for so long called for a vote and thereby a say in the form and application of the laws under which the nation lived. 'The law has triumphed,' said Kydd and McCrae, 'but has it changed that widespread distress that knows no limits [and which] has penetrated the home of every workman in the land?' The answer to that would soon become clear to anyone who picked up London's *Morning Chronicle* and read the reports of Henry Mayhew's survey of life in London in these years; that is, life in London for the hundreds of thousands who just managed to feed themselves. The laws of Britain were not formed for London's fruit-sellers, clothesmen, organ boys, singers, crossing sweepers, water-carriers, bone-grubbers and rag-gatherers, pure-finders and cigar-end finders, sewer-hunters and mud-larks of the Jewish, the Irish, the Italian and every other nationality represented in London. Of the 'beggar street-sellers' Mayhew says:

'Under this heading I include only such of the beggar street-sellers as are neither infirm nor suffering from any severe bodily affliction or privation. I am well aware that the aged – the blind – the lame and the halt often *pretend* to sell small articles in the street – such as boot laces, tracts, cabbage-nets, lucifer-matches, kettle-holders, and the like; and that such matters are carried by them partly to keep clear of the law, and partly to evince a disposition to the public that they are willing to do something for their livelihood. Such, though beggars, are not 'lurkers' – a lurker being strictly one who loiters about for some dishonest purpose.'[179]

These beggar-street people did not count even in Chartist calculations of who would benefit from a parliament voted in by a universal male franchise. As to the crossing-sweepers found in most of London's streets and squares, they did the work 'either on account of their bodily afflictions...or because the occupation is the last resource left to them of earning a living, and they considered even the scanty subsistence it yields preferable to that of the workhouse.'[180]

James Bezer understood the revulsion of the workhouse which he described as, 'that worst of all prisons so dreaded by the poor.' By his own account he managed always to avoid entering his local workhouse at Whitechapel yet seems to have been intimate enough with it to know it helped those in sudden need but reviled long term paupers. 'Once an outcast, mind what you're at: if you are only hungry six hours, why they'll give you [something] to eat, but if hungry six months, O, starve away, or beg, or steal, there's plenty of workhouses and jails for such obstinate burdens, and we pay rates, and very heavily too, to keep them out of our sight. God save the Queen!'[181]

Bezer's compatriot and leading London Chartist William Cuffay whose African grandfather had been taken from that country on a slave ship to the Americas in the mid-1700s, worked all his life as a tailor in and around the Strand and Soho. Cuffay was, then, one-rung up the social ladder from James Bezer though probably flourishing little better. His wife Mary was five years his junior, fifty-five to her husband's sixty years. They had married at St James, Piccadilly in 1827 and now lodged in Soho. Cuffay was physically small, probably because of rickets, but was politically of greater determination than many of his Chartist colleagues. As a London tailor he was not unused to action in support of social improvement; the tailors were organised and had held out, unsuccessfully, for better wages and shorter hours in 1834. As a leading Chartist, Cuffay regretted the actions of 10th April when the petition had been left on Kennington Common. On that day he had urged the people to keep to their planned march upon the Houses of Parliament because he felt the soldiers' bayonets should be faced to show that this was how the government maintained its control. Kennington Common would be a turning-point for him, as for a good many Chartists.

With leading Chartists Ernest Jones in prison and Peter McDouall awaiting his trial in Lancashire, it was left to others of the likes of William Cuffay and James Bezer to continue the fight. By early August, Cuffay was attending the secret meetings of the Ulterior Committee which had kept to its course after the disappointment of June when Peter McDouall had abandoned the revolutionary plan. James Beezer seems to have stepped-back from the cabal but there were many others across London prepared to stand 'shoulder by shoulder'. A rising was in the planning. The most prominent of the conspirators were William Cuffay; George Mullins the twenty-two-year-old surgeon's apprentice; bootmaker William Lacey; James Bassett who had been a Chartist delegate in April and one of the June conspirators, and two others, Payne and Brewster. Another prominent member of this cabal was Joseph Richie, bricklayer, who lived with Ann Haydon in a kitchen at 2 Cross Court, Russell Court, off Drury Lane, an area identified by Friedrich Engels as one of the worst in London. Richie was a Chartist class-leader. There was another member, highly significant: Thomas Powell, Hoxton carpenter and government spy who had found his way into the group through an unwitting James Bezer. Thomas Powell was known to his companions as 'Johnson' and, like George Davis who also regularly attended these meetings, was passing information on to his police contact.

The two surviving Chartist Association Executives, Samuel Kydd and John McCrae, seem to have known what was in the planning. Samuel Kydd passed to George Mullins or James Bassett a message from the Manchester Chartists who were seeking to coordinate with London's organisers in the rising to come.[182] William Lacey was dispatched north to liaise.

August was turning out to be a wet month. The men of the Ulterior Committee who met on the evening of Tuesday 15th August 1848, at The Lord Denham beer shop across the river from the city in Great Suffolk Street, Southwark, might well have arrived damp for they would, almost certainly, have come on foot, perhaps through rain, from their various locations. Cuffay was there, Richie was there, Brewster, Mullins, Payne, and the spies Powell and Davis. These meetings had been going on fairly consistently since early June but tonight's meeting was different. William Lacey's return from the north had been expected for twenty-four hours, and finally, after eluding a police tail, he arrived at The Lord Denham. Lacey's news was that Birmingham and Manchester were 'up and doing.'[183] Manchester and the surrounding towns of Hyde, Ashton, Heywood and Dukenfield were said to be waiting for a signal for a simultaneous rising. Unbeknownst to the Ulterior Committee, the Home Office had already received an alert from Oldham's magistrates of a Chartist plan to march on Manchester 'for the avowed purpose of burning the town and shooting the Magistrates – that the rising [is] to be general throughout the Kingdom and that Ernest Jones [is] to be liberated.'[184] The time had come. The Londoners must make their move and it was decided for the very next night.

The earlier urgings of Peter McDouall to organise, the warnings from Ernest Jones that it was up to each man to prepare were showing results of a kind. At the Lord Denham the remaining members of the Ulterior Committee planned together for the following night's momentous action. It was moved by George

Mullins that 'each delegate should go back to his locality and pick four men out who were willing to do anything that was required of them.' Someone wanted to know exactly what was meant by that so the young man pointed to the gas flame by way of demonstration. This was to 'mince the matter' so far as the older William Cuffay was concerned. They knew, he said, that their necks were in jeopardy; in fact, 'the halter was round their necks, and it was no use to say it in half words...they wanted men to fire [police] station-houses, or warehouses, or anything that might be required of them.'[185] Mustering points in the eastern districts of London were settled upon, tasks delegated. It was agreed that the next afternoon, before the operation began, Richie would meet with his class members at the Orange Tree beer-shop in Red Lion Square; the Southwark contingent was to meet at the Angel pub on Webber Street. From these locations they would proceed to their areas of action which was set for ten o'clock the following night. As everyone went back to their homes, they went knowing that tomorrow would be a day never forgotten. And for them it never was. Most would be behind bars within a few hours but that in no way reflects upon their undoubted seriousness. They were part of a national rising; organisation was as good as could be; timing was as coordinated as the times allowed; the decision was made.

Four key points in London had been chosen by the Ulterior Committee: The Seven Dials which lies between Leicester Square and Covent Garden; Strutton Ground, a half-mile south-east of Buckingham Palace at Westminster; Clerkenwell Green; and Tower Hamlets. This was a wide area of action. The Chartist groups in these areas were supposed to be organised along the lines recommended by Peter McDouall: the districts, localities, the wards and sections, so that the August 1848 revolutionaries would have their wards of 100 men in each. The men of Marylebone, Paddington, Somers Town and Chelsea were to proceed to The Seven Dials and Dean Street, those from the south London areas were to meet at Westminster. It was expected that they would come armed, with pikes, blades of some kind or guns. The Birmingham police inspector Charles Field was still sending lists to the Home Office of guns sent to London, and William Cuffay was one

Londoner who possessed a firearm. A select group of forty-six men were to go with Joseph Richie to cause blazes. This would create panic and let other groups know that action had begun; it loosely accords with the tactics planned for the aborted June plot. Gunsmiths' shops could be raided for arms. Once the insurrection was under way, the leaders would be identified by the wristbands they wore. These were the basics of the operation planned for the night time hours of Wednesday 16th and early morning hours of Thursday 17th August 1848. Who would be Britain's Lamartine if insurrection became successful revolution is a moot point. As Ernest Jones was to be released from his prison cell, it is he probably who would have found himself elevated to that position.

Immediately after the Lord Denham meeting the police informer Thomas Powell took the London conspirators' plans to the Metropolitan Police, thence to the Home Office. The authorities waited a full eighteen hours before putting their counter operations into action which took place early on the evening of Wednesday 16th. They left the conspirators to go about their business for the entire of that day while ensuring the military at Buckingham Palace, the Tower, Mint, Bank of England, 'and the various barracks' were under arms.[186] The police closed in on the conspirators only as evening drew in, presumably in order to apprehend them as they grouped with incriminating weaponry and combustibles upon them. Through the information given by Powell, police officers of Kensington's F Division, led by Superintendent Pearce, entered the Orange Tree beer-shop at Red Lion Square at six o'clock. This body of officers went up to the first floor, quietly, to a room at the front of the building and surprised Joseph Richie and the ten men with him all talking around a table. Richie and his colleagues had by this time prepared fire-balls to cause the blazing of buildings. These articles were in a bag tied up in a blue handkerchief and smelling strongly of turpentine.[187] Pearce frisked Richie and found two large daggers on him, then ordered that his residence, the kitchen at No. 2, Cross-court, Russell-court, Drury Lane, be searched. All eleven men were taken into custody.

Three hours later, the light now all but gone, armed police officers of Lambeth's L Division, led by Superintendent Anthony

Rutt and reinforced with men from P division, executed much the same operation across the river at the Angel public house on Webber Street Southwark, but this time it was in the ground-floor tap room that they found thirteen leading conspirators. Superintendent Rutt entered with his cutlass drawn and there threatened to cut down anyone who moved. The apprehended men were searched. One was found with a pistol, primed and loaded. Gunpowder was discovered. The prisoners were charged in front of the Angel's lobby then taken to Tower Street police station under a large escort of officers. An hour or two later some six hundred Confederates were reported to be making their way from Moor Street down to Southwark. They had heard about the police raid there. A small group of them was confronted by the police at a public house, possibly the Webber Street establishment. The Confederates were armed but disappeared at the sight of the police force's cutlasses.[188]

By this time, getting on for ten o'clock at night, a large crowd had gathered in the streets of The Seven Dials as pre-arranged. As their leaders had not arrived it was probably not too difficult a task for the police to clear the streets, which they did. The police continued with raids in Westminster where more arrests were made by officers of Westminster's A Division at Blue Anchor yard off York Street, location of the Irish Confederate Curran Club, and at a coffee-house run by William Lacey at Strutton Ground. Towards midnight a young man called Henry Argue was apprehended across town, on Bow Street itself, a gun concealed under his coat and upon him an Irish Felon Society membership card, inscribed with 'the last words of Mitchel.'[189] This heralded the end of the revolutionary hopes of 1848 in England, although there was more to come in Ireland.

James Bezer was arrested at this time, not for involvement in the Ulterior Committee plot (which would become known as the Orange Tree Plot) although he had attended at least one of their meetings, but for his speech given at the Milton Street theatre at the time of the Irish rising. He and his wife Jane had six young children, one a new-born. Many more arrests had already been made at Liverpool, Oldham, Manchester and Bolton, all by police forces with the exception of Ashton-under-Lyne where military action was needed.

In light of the efficiency and coolness with which the authorities dealt with it, the revolutionary attempt of August 1848 might seem a delusional affair but it was in the planning for weeks, its scope was national, and it meant everything to the thousands of men and women across the country who tried it, to the men imprisoned for it and to those left alone in its wake. Betrayal by informers and the difficulty of communication between parties were two great stumbling blocks, yet the organisation was there, and the will. Had they succeeded in any degree to carry out their plans, parts of London would have been ablaze and men, women and children exposed to the consequences. David Goodway says: '[t]he conspiracy of 1848 was not only the last of the revolutionary attempts which originated in the 1790s; it was also the one based on the greatest degree of support in London.'[190] It is safe to say that the night of August 16th 1848 represents a Britain gripped by a class war in which men from bricklayers to shop assistants, surgeon's apprentices to bakers sought to bring about change to an elitist society which they had come to believe would never change unless forced.

12
Hearings and Trials

'We earnestly recommend all persons in the great towns of the kingdom, who in any way may have become informed of the haunts or proceedings of these pothouse conspirators, to give timely warning to the police. The rest may safely be left to the public authorities.' So printed *The Times* on the morning of 18th August 1848.[191] At eleven o'clock on the morning following the arrests, Thomas J. Hall, chief magistrate at Bow Street, examined the twenty-three men taken at the Orange Tree and the Angel public houses. A *Morning Chronicle* reporter said the prisoners appeared to be below 'ordinary physical strength,' and their faces did not show 'any of that ferocity of disposition which the atrocious character of the crime imputed to them would seem naturally to betoken.'[192]

The lawyer James Macnmara had arrived at the magistrates' court to represent the twenty-three prisoners. This would be another example of the examinations of Chartists which he had attended at Bow Street magistrates' court over the past few weeks. Upon his arrival he was refused access to his clients unless in the presence of an inspector, and so he entered the court room ignorant of the exact charges to which his clients must answer but it became clear enough when Mr Clarkson, for the Crown, suggested they might be tried for treason. In his cross-examination of police Superintendent Pearce of F Division, Macnmara put it to him that the prisoners had made no attempt to conceal themselves or the fire-balls said to be found with them at the Orange Tree. Any suggestion that the fire-balls might have been planted by the police was refuted by Superintendent Pearce. The young lawyer's task was not an easy one. In Joseph Richie's room more than one hundred ball cartridges had been found, also bullet moulds and what looked like combustible balls. Powder and a powder-horn also were found, and 'a bottle of gunpowder, a bayonet, a ladle for melting lead, a quantity of tow, some percussion caps and some small shot.'[193] The only mitigation which Macnmara could extract from the police witness to these discoveries at Richie's room at Cross-Court, Russell-Court,

Drury Lane, was that he did not know for certain that Richie lived there.

A laugh was raised in court when Superintendent Rutt who had made the arrests at the Angel public house in Southwark described his swash-buckling entry into the tap-room. 'I went in with a cutlass in one hand and a pistol in the other; and I said, "The first man who dares resist, or even lift his hand up, I'll cut him down or fire at him."' But the evidence which had been found that night, the daggers, swords, pistols and pike heads two feet long, would have been viewed by the court more soberly.

And then the informer Thomas Powell was brought in. With the defendants present the atmosphere at his appearance must have been electric. From this time on Powell was obliged to go about under police protection and to have his house guarded. He identified Joseph Richie and the Confederate William Lacey to the court. It was now, during Macnmara's cross-examination of Powell, that a sensational admission was heard in the magistrates' court. While explaining to Macnmara his role in the whole affair, of his involvement with the Chartists and his attendance at the Ulterior Committee's meetings, Powell said, 'I encouraged these men on. I did so on purpose, in order to inform against them.'[194] Despite this home goal, his testimony would condemn the prisoners. For the time being they were remanded in custody for a fortnight pending trial. Bail was not allowed.

That was on the morning of Thursday 17th August. On the evening of the following day William Cuffay was arrested at his home in Soho. Mary Cuffay was there with him when police constable William Cross came into their room, a 'garret' he called it. Cuffay was charged with felony and conspiring against the Queen. 'I understand what I am charged with,' was Cuffay's response. The policeman said that his prisoner then opened a drawer, fumbled about in it for a moment, found the article he was looking for, a pistol, and made to pass it to his wife. There was a struggle between police officer and Cuffay, perhaps not a serious one – Cuffay was under five feet tall – as the weapon was taken from him. It was later said to be loaded with gunpowder and ball, and primed. A Chartist flag from the Westminster District, which had seen some service at various demonstrations that year and which William Cuffay cherished, was also found and taken away. Presumably, all that was left to Mary Cuffay was to alert her husband's colleagues to what had happened. Very probably James Macnmara was called out again to Bow Street that night, or the next morning, to act for the prisoner. A pikestaff was later found in the cockloft of Cuffay's building.[195] Pikes sound archaic but they were feared by mounted soldiers and police. A rider and his horse were highly vulnerable to a man wielding a pike, especially in an urban setting. In the streets of London, a pike would be a fearsome weapon.

The Chartist National Association was prepared for arrests of its members. It had a Central Victim and Defence Committee which met at Soho premises on Dean Street but by the end of August so many Chartists had been arrested in London and in the northern towns that legal costs were spiralling out of control. The Executive was already appealing to the country for more money for its own administration while national events had reached a point beyond the Association's ability to pay for the defence of men arrested. James Macnmara's fees alone exceeded £300; that for work just in London. On the eve of his trial Peter McDouall's Defence Fund had received less than £3 excluding donations from Ashton-under-Lyne, and 'unless our Chartist friends in the country will bestir themselves and forward subscriptions, [we] fear we shall not be able to take witnesses down to Liverpool,' warned the fund's administrators.[196]

Peter McDouall's trial had finally arrived. On Monday, 28th August, ten days after William Cuffay's arrest, McDouall, who had been out on bail for four weeks, appeared at Liverpool's Crown Court to answer to the charge of 'uttering seditious language.' When Thomas Lacey had gone from London to liaise with the northern Chartists and Confederate clubs, he had expected to meet McDouall who surely knew, two weeks before his trial opened, that the Chartist groups which he had principally organised were about to launch an insurrectionary action across the country. It must have gone through his mind how success would free him from having to appear as a defendant at Liverpool's Crown Court on that Monday morning. And it was not just his future which was at stake. Mary Anne

McDouall was in the last stages of pregnancy and she and her husband already had three very young children.

Peter McDouall is described in the *Liverpool Mercury* as an 'intelligent looking man.' The prosecution laid importance on this. The Attorney General, John Jervis, gave the opinion that the prisoner was 'not an ignorant man, like those he addressed, but a man of talent, of considerable powers of eloquence, and likely to [impress] the ignorant people he was addressing.' It is reported that at Ashton-under-Lyne, McDouall had told a crowd that the soldiers would turn against their masters and that 'before the harvest was finished,' he could promise them the six points of the Charter, and something more; the 'something more' being simply expressed with the words: "organize, organize, organize!"[197] McDouall was standing behind the bar as corrupter, as a Machiavellian inciter to treasonable acts which the British worker, if left alone, never would contemplate.

Years before, when practising as a medical doctor, Peter McDouall had seen things in the small factory towns of Lancashire which ever after propelled him upon the path which had brought him to this point. In the 1830s he had witnessed enough of the lives of the factory workers to make him publicly denounce the practices of their employers. It made him a pariah among them. Now, after ten years as a Chartist leader, he had arrived at the point again of imprisonment and ruin; and this time danger to his family. He was sentenced to two years at Kirkdale Gaol. Life would never again be the same for Peter McDouall and his family and to his legal advisor W.P. Roberts at the close of his trial, he expressed great anxiety for his wife and children.[198]

The arrests of Chartists and Confederates from June to September 1848 were many and possibly touched every community in the land. Those arrested ranged from two boys at Bingley in Yorkshire, (Smith and Kelvington, who had been entertaining themselves with military-like manoeuvres which escalated into a full scale military movement of actual soldiers through the zeal of a local magistrate) to the mass national arrests of men seriously intent on revolution.[199] Newspaper concentration tended to be on the prosecutions of leading figures but the process was felt no less by the boys Smith and Kelvington as by Chartists Ernest Jones and Peter McDouall. The law overwhelmed them all – the very law which the Chartists wanted to reform through a parliamentary vote. By 1848, a great many of the working families willing to stand with the Chartist or Confederate leadership had reached the point where they were prepared to break the law to gain a voice, and they declared it legitimate to do so. But it was a contradiction in terms, said the judge while summing up at Peter McDouall's trial, 'to say that it could be lawful to break the law. If it were lawful to resist a law, there must be another law that allowed it.' This was the extent of the logic used by Peter McDouall's judge to demonstrate that the Chartist position was, thereby, 'an absurdity.'[200] By such logic as this, upper and many middle-class people permitted themselves not to face the reality of life for working families or consider any other moral law which might apply.

On the day Peter McDouall was tried at Liverpool, 28th August 1848, James Bezer was tried for sedition before Mr Baron Platt at London's Central Criminal Court. Although the lawyer James Macnmara was continuing to represent prisoners who did not have counsel, he did not assist at James Bezer's trial. Bezer defended himself. The prosecutor admonished the prisoner for having read out to the Milton Street assembly, on 28th July, inflammatory extracts from the *New York Herald* with the intention of 'exciting his listeners to violence' and thinking himself safe in doing so – this was a device which would not save him from the law. Bezer responded by saying that anyone could read *The Times* in which the extracts appeared, so *The Times* should be prosecuted for printing it in the first place. This riposte was too clever and went to prove the defendant's 'dangerous ability' to sway the minds of others. The jury returned a verdict of guilty. Baron Platt felt himself duty bound to make an example of Bezer and his companions James Maxwell Bryson and the Confederate Robert Crowe, by sentencing each to two years' imprisonment. Because Robert Crowe had been charged upon the evidence of one policeman, it took the jury two hours to find him guilty. '[I]t would be better in such cases to have the evidence of two witnesses,' the foreman told the court. Baron Platt agreed but said that 'such a course was not always practicable.' At sentencing, one newspaper reporter thought the prisoners appeared 'thoroughly dejected and crestfallen,' though Bryson tried to cheer the others with 'Never mind, brother Chartists, come along,' before they left the courtroom.[201]

Robert Crowe, who had responded so excitedly at the time of the Irish rising, was sent to Tothill Bridewell and would spend much of his time in a cell next to Ernest Jones. Bezer was kept at Newgate and says he was visited more than once whilst there by one of the local magistrates who had commanded the defences of one of the city's bridges on 10th April. The alderman thought Bezer a fool who had brought himself and others into trouble, and he went on to tell his prisoner that it was as well the Chartists and Confederates had not attempted to march on parliament on the day of the Kennington Common meeting as they 'would all have been annihilated.'[202]

13
The Prisoners

Deadly blows had been dealt the Chartist and the Confederate associations by John Russell's Whig government. Much the same was happening across the Channel. In France, 'nothing but curses' had been heard against the Socialist Louis Blanc since the bloody days in Paris of 23rd to 26th June, and by mid-September he had joined the many exiles and émigrés living in London. But he left behind a France whose men now voted in a representative of their choice to the Chamber of Deputies, through a universal male franchise. A newly created French Presidency was also subject to the male vote while whosoever was elected to the office was to have unilateral control of the military. This latter arrangement was one which Louis Napoleon would make good use of before another year was out, after he was elected President – but that was not for another three months. And in northern Italy the forces of the small but bold state of Piedmont had finally been defeated by the Austrian forces of Josef Radetzky. The Pope was supposed to have supported the military campaign in the north against the Austrians but withdrew his troops. Giuseppe Garibaldi, some time since arrived in Italy from Montevideo, remained prepared to fight the Austrians until, in mid-August, he was obliged to accept defeat – for now.

In London, George Julian Harney, who had greeted the news of the French Revolution of February with such great delight, was now accusing the revolutionary French government of plundering French citizens in the name of 'Equality', denying them the rights of free speech and free writing in the name of 'Liberty', and exiling them in the name of 'Fraternity', but he conceded that at least the working men of France had the suffrage which no working man in Britain had or looked likely ever to have.[203] By September 1848, after all that had happened in the previous four months, his spring-time euphoria had quite dissolved away. But at least he was not in a prison cell. He had chosen his job at the *Northern Star* over a seat on the Chartist Assembly of May 1848. Had he played his part in the National Assembly of May might he have backed Ernest Jones to the point of imprisonment? Might he have conspired with Peter McDouall in June?

Back in 1842, when the unprecedented national strike was in full force, Harney had kept his adopted town of Sheffield from industrial sabotage and rioting because he had come to the conclusion, after his dagger wielding of three years earlier, that insurrection was useless unless it was organised and likely to come to something. In 1842 he had seen that the great march of strikers from one northern town to another, the smashing of boiler plugs, the military actions in the streets and the deaths which followed, would come to nothing, and he had been right. The demonstrators and marchers were in no fit state to raise a revolution, constitutional or forceful; the Chartist body was not fit to organise it. 1848 though, was different. With revolutions coming to something in so many of the continental countries and with endeavours to organise at home bearing fruit, Harney seems briefly, wildly, to have hoped for political change in Britain, perhaps even through a rising. Yet two years earlier he had written to Friedrich Engels: 'To organize, to conspire a revolution in this country would be a vain and foolish project and the men who with their eyes open could take part in so absurd an attempt would be worse than foolish, would be highly culpable.'[204] Believing that the people of Britain would never rise, his mental scope instead encompassed a European wide socialist revolution. But in large part the continental revolutions of 1848 had been inspired by a sense of nationhood; they were 'bourgeois' says historian Peter Watson, not socialistic.[205] By the summer of 1848 the socialist movement in France had collapsed and others were not to last. For the duration of 1848 Julian Harney kept to his desk at the printing offices at Great Windmill Street, he kept to his wife Mary and their children at their home in Queen Street, Brompton, and he kept to his hopes of an 'unceasing, gradual, peaceable, and resolute aggressive popular movement.'[206] His association with Friedrich Engels and Karl Marx continued.

And so, in 1848 Julian Harney did not experience Tothill Bridewell, where Ernest Jones, Alexander Sharp, Joseph Williams, John Fussell and William John Vernon were taken after their sentencing in July. All but Joseph Williams had been delegates at the April Convention, and Sharp, Vernon and Jones had been National Assembly members. Tothill Bridewell stood east of Vauxhall Bridge Road in Westminster, not far from Buckingham Palace. Westminster Cathedral stands there now. It was a new set of buildings arranged in circular form so that warders could oversee its inmates' activities from a central point. Ernest Jones was kept there between July 1848 and July 1850 – the fates of others differed. He lived out his days in a cell twelve feet by seven feet, 'locked up in solitude and silence.' The silent system in the prisons of 1848 had something to do with religious reflection but was, in reality, a punishment beyond imagining. He says his night cell was nine feet by four feet with a loosely-shuttered and unglazed window and there he slept on a bed of straw covered with a piece of carpeting. During a time of extra punishment, he was confined alone in a darkened cell without heat. The food might have been enough to keep a body alive, but the cold must have been terrible. Through two bitter winters he rose each day at five o'clock, crossed two yards in shirt and trousers to wash and dress in the open air. For two winters he sat, after his morning ablutions, in damp clothes in a fireless cell.[207] That he, and many like him, survived this existence is hard to comprehend. Some did not. 'Stick a man in the dock and call him "Chartist," that is enough; the brutal *bourgeoisie* will howl unanimously "Away with him, away with him! Crucify him! Crucify him!"'[208]

The Chartist prisoners at Tothill quickly came to believe that Home Secretary George Grey had ordered their especially cruel treatment. Within a month of their imprisonment, on 25th August, MP Thomas Wakley raised this in the House of Commons. George Grey assured the House that all prisoners were classed by magistrates 'subject to the approval of the Secretary of State, under Act of Parliament,' and that he had no authority to alter the regulations under which prisoners lived.[209] In fact it was stated by another in the House during the same session that the prisoners' treatment was lenient, that 'every indulgence' was being given. They were allowed books, subject to the prison chaplain's approval, their diet comprised white bread, cocoa and gruel, six ounces of meat and eight ounces of potato four times a week, soup instead of meat on the remaining three days. But it was the case that the local magistrates held arbitrary power over the Tothill Fields prisoners.

At this time, the Irish nationalist John Mitchel, the inspiration of so much fury and activity before, during and after his trial and transportation in May, had arrived at the penal colony in Bermuda on the war steamer *The Scourge*. A rumour was spreading in London that he had a servant to wait upon him and was living a better life than 'many of the officers in Her Majesty's service on that island.' George Grey said that 'no such information had reached the Government and he was certain...that it was not correct.'[210] Mitchel's own records suggest that it painted an exaggerated picture.[211]

Meanwhile, at Dublin's Kilmainham prison, William Smith O'Brien, Thomas Meagher and Terence McManus were awaiting their October trials to be held at Clonmel in County Tipperary. This was O'Brien and Meagher's second trial of 1848 at the hands of the English justice system. Here at Kilmainham they were kept while Lucy Smith O'Brien brought them their daily meal. But not every one of Ireland's leading Confederates was incarcerated in her prisons. Some had managed to escape arrest. Michael Doheny, delegate at the London National Assembly of May and still living as a fugitive in Ireland, was about to join John O'Mahony in a renewed revolutionary attempt.

John O'Mahony, he who had brought the men to William Smith O'Brien at Carrick at the start of the rising in July, again gathered his men in late August 1848. 'No man,' wrote Michael Doheny, 'was ever followed with truer devotion or served with more unwavering fidelity.'[212] In the last week of August, a crowd was seen ascending Aheny Hill about five miles to the north of Carrick in Tipperary. Another camp appeared near the village of Portlaw. By 13th September news of the preliminary activities of the rebels was filtering through to London's newspaper readers. Although parliament was in recess, the Home Office and government would be fully apprised of all that was going on, but London's general public might easily have missed it at first. What was going on in Kilkenny and Waterford was everything necessary to provide for a revolutionary army, and in a much more practical manner than had been followed by Smith O'Brien. Smith O'Brien had ordered no intrusion upon private property, no cutting down of trees for defence purposes, no taking of provisions unless paid for. O'Mahony's men were not impeded by such scruples and were ready to proceed upon their work. 'The time between the first step in revolution and action is the most trying,' Michael Doheny later wrote. Some of O'Mahony's men were killed during preliminary incursions, but it was the failure of reinforcements from Kilkenny to arrive which seems to have beaten the heart out of the rising. After three days of waiting, the forces dispersed. On the night of 16th September, O'Mahony, in a state of undress, fled his house and rode off only minutes ahead of an arresting party of police.[213] A price was put on his head and he, like the rest, became a fugitive. He managed to reach the relative safety of Wales before making it to France.

In London, by September 1848, great numbers of men had been tried and imprisoned but not all. Some still awaited their trials. After his arrest in his Soho garret, the tailor William Cuffay had been kept at Newgate in the weeks before his trial which finally opened on 25th September at the Central Criminal Court at the Old Bailey. He faced his prosecutors together with William Lacey, Thomas Fay, and the London Confederate William Dowling. All were found guilty under the new Treason Felony Act of levying war against the Queen and her government, and were sentenced, on 30th September to life transportation. At the moment of sentence, Thomas Fay, just twenty years old, exclaimed to the court, 'this is the baptism of felony in England,' then he looked up to the gallery from where the viewing public, surely members of his family, looked down. 'Good-bye, my flowers,' he said, 'good-bye, fellow countrymen.'[214] They were taken to Millbank Penitentiary until their ship sailed.

More from the 16th August Orange Tree arrests were tried at this time. On 2nd October came the turn of Joseph Richie who was sentenced at the Central Criminal Court to life transportation. One of Richie's companions in the dock was a young man called William Scadding. Scadding worked as a brass turner, came from a secure artisan family and had been married three years to an Irish woman called Elizabeth Benson. The week before her husband was sentenced to imprisonment at Tothill Fields Bridewell, Elizabeth brought their second son into the world at their home, a ground-floor back room at 31, Cock Lane, Smithfield. They called him William Daniel.

George Mullins, the leading conspirator who had pointed to the flaming gas light at the Lord Denham public house on the eve of the attempted August rising, managed to elude arrest for a full month. He was eventually found on the night of Monday 18th September, not at his home at 34 Southampton Street off the Strand but in the cellar of his father's house in Tatham Court, John Street, close by the Old Kent Road. In his attempt to escape Mullins had dressed as a woman, in his mother's clothes according to a witness, with veil and bonnet. James Macnmara was again brought in as legal representative but two days later Mullins seemed abandoned, no James Macnmara in sight, when he stood alone before the magistrates at Bow Street and was charged with conspiring to levy war against the Queen and her government. He said he was 'wholly unprepared for his defence.'[215] The spy Robert Powell was there though, to give evidence against him and George Mullins was held over until his trial which would not take place for another six weeks.

By now the Chartist Defence Fund was not able to meet its financial commitments to men like James Macnmara. Feargus O'Connor had hoped all London's Chartist prisoners would be legally represented and to this end he was, apparently, subsidising the Defence Fund from his own pocket. It is quite likely that Macnmara, after three months of hectic activity at Bow Street and the Central Criminal Court, was cooling in ardour towards his work for the Chartist prisoners: it is likely that his legal fees were not being paid by the time of George Mullins's arrest. At some point Feargus O'Connor, aware of the immense work and consequent cost incurred by the Defence Fund in representing the endless queue of arrested Chartists, and presumably alarmed at the cost to himself, wrote to his young friend instructing him to take work only at his say-so. This was a mistake because, twelve months later, James Macnmara sued O'Connor for money owed.

It was left to individual efforts to support the families of the imprisoned men. During the two years of his incarceration at Tothill

Bridewell, the family of Ernest Jones was supported by the people of Halifax. London made early efforts to provide for James Bezer's wife Jane and six children when the Milton Street theatre, scene of Bezer's fateful speech, hosted a benefit on Tuesday 26th September intending to put Jane Bezer into some sort of business. A charge of two pence for the boxes and platform, and one pence for the pit and gallery were generally asked for to fund 'the victims' but the weather on this occasion was so wet that very few attended.[216] What happened to the families of the more obscure Chartist prisoners is left to the imagination.

John Russell's Whig government and the British parliament could consider their campaign against the insurgents well planned and executed. The prime minister liked to think of Chartism as got up by 'designing and insidious persons'; that the people were manipulated by men like Peter McDouall and Ernest Jones for their own base sinister purposes.[217] He and those of similar mind saw only the ruin of 'all the ancient foundations' of society were Chartism to have its universal franchise.[218] John Russell should have consulted with the street fish seller James Bezer who, when a young man, had begun to question why so many should starve while a few lived in luxury: 'And so, Lord John, I became a Rebel; – that is to say: – Hungry in a land of plenty. I began seriously for the first time in my life to enquire WHY, WHY – a dangerous question, Lord John, isn't it, for a poor man to ask? leading to anarchy and confusion.'[219]

14
The Middle-Class Element

And yet back in 1831, when James Bezer was but thirteen years old, Lord John Russell appeared to be acting in a manner which the East End teenager would very likely have applauded. Earlier in his political career, Russell was Paymaster General in Lord Grey's 1830-1832 Whig government and he was charged in 1831 with preparing a Reform Bill to present to parliament. One purpose of this Bill was to replace aristocratic parliamentary control with one which would be subject to the influence of the rising middle classes. To bring the reforms about all the strategies later employed by Feargus O'Connor and many other of the Chartist leaders, the intimations of violence and risings, were used by the 1831 Reform Bill's supporters – and not threats alone. The Duke of Wellington's house was attacked, thousands marched on the King to press for reform, there were riots in Nottingham and Derby and then, spectacularly, in October 1831 Bristol was set alight. In the House of Commons, Russell was accused of encouraging breaches of the peace through 'persons who set themselves in array against the Legislature of the country.'[220] Then, on 25th January 1832, a letter from the Home Office bore clear evidence that insurrection would be tolerated if that was what was needed to bring parliament to reform.[221] A boy like James Bezer, doing all to survive in the streets of London, might well have idolised Russell at this point but there was bitter disappointment ahead.

The Whig's strategies triumphed and the Great Reform Act, promisingly called the Representation of the People Act, was passed in June 1832. The parliament which followed, led by a large majority Whig government brought in on the votes of the newly enfranchised middle classes, was supposed by the working classes to be friendly towards them. From the outset the reformed parliament showed itself to be anything but. This Whig government, under Charles Grey, brought in coercive legislation for Ireland (the Suppression of Disturbances Act) which dealt a near fatal blow to the faith put in it by the working classes, and then in 1834 came the 'hideous and accurst New Poor Law, which tears asunder the dearest and holiest Ties of the human Heart, which consigns even the Old and infirm to FAMISH amid the Gloom and SOLITUDE of a Dungeon Workhouse.'[222] The effects of this latter on any who feared ending up in a workhouse cannot be overstated for it separated man from wife, parent from child and replaced care for those unable to work with a regime design to punish. It was the New Poor Law which destroyed all working-class confidence in successive Whig governments and their middle-class supporters.

By 1848 Douglas Jerrold, Henry Mayhew's father-in-law, was moved to write: 'The mechanics and artisans were not only forgotten by those whom they had contributed to raise to power [in 1831-1832], but their remonstrances were laughed at, and their [Chartist] petitions spurned.'[223] Yet, even as the great crowds were making their way home from Kennington Common on 10th April 1848 after their vain attempt to bring pressure to bear upon the Whig led parliament, one middle-class parliamentarian spoke out in the House of Commons in support of a further extension of voting rights. This was John Bright, thirty-seven-years-old, a Rochdale mill owner and Quaker who, on that day, reminded the House that it represented only one out of every seven grown males in Britain.[224]

Within five days of the Kennington Common meeting, some fifty parliamentarians favouring constitutional reform had established a New Reform Movement. This new movement was led by Scotsman Joseph Hume and its principles were in almost every respect those of Chartism's.[225] In fact its terms were soon being called the Little Charter. But there was one great divide between the middle-class movement and the working-class Chartists: the middle classes would only support household suffrage, that is the extension of voting rights to those who paid rent for a house to a certain sum; the Chartist body would accept no compromise on an unconditional universal male vote.[226] But it was the lack of trust felt by the working classes in their erstwhile middle-class compatriots after the 1831 campaign which was the real issue and because of this the Chartist Executive felt that anything less than a universal male franchise was a weak and unsafe way forward. Feargus O'Connor had been adamant on this point for years.

Even so, as the great London disturbances of late-May and early-June 1848 broke out, the debate on class cooperation went on and, a little over two weeks later on 20th June, the elderly Joseph Hume stood up in the House of Commons and said that the 1832 Reform Act 'had not effected all the objects for which he had struggled at the time, and which the country, from one end to the other, had interested itself to obtain.'[227]

'Out of the 5,000,000 or 6,000,000 male adults above twenty-one, which there are in this country, taking the average, some individuals being registered for more than three, four, or five different places, the number of registered electors does not amount to more than from 800,000 or 850,000. All the remainder then of the 5,000,000 or 6,000,000 adults who have not that privilege, are placed in an inferior situation, and deprived of that right which by the constitution they are entitled to enjoy.'[228]

Parliament was not performing as it should. At present the working people were slaves with 'a master to make laws for him and to direct him,' they were not freemen with a voice in the constitution.

'[T]his House, as at present constituted, does not fairly represent the population, the property, or the industry of the Country...and it is therefore expedient, with a view to amend the National Representation, that the Elective Franchise shall be so extended as to include all Householders—that votes shall be taken by Ballot—that the duration of Parliaments shall not exceed three years—and that the apportionment of [Parliament's] Members to Population shall be made more equal.'[229]

Most significantly, during this debate John Russell back-pedalled on his position on reform. He said he had been misrepresented, that he had never said the people did not want reform but that he had said the middle and working classes wanted 'gradual process in reform.' Hume challenged this interpretation. Russell, after a lengthy speech, conceded that 'a time may come – perhaps it is not too distant – when reforms...may be usefully introduced and carried into effect for the improvement of the representation.'[230] The conspirators of the Chartist-Confederate Ulterior Committee were at this very time meeting in various London coffee and beer houses and though there might be talk of reform in the Houses of Parliament they had entirely given up on that: by now revolution was their purpose.

The Little Charter came to nothing but in the following sixteen months, while the prisoners of 1848 were serving their time in the gaols of Britain, a Parliamentary and Financial Reform League was formed by Sir Joshua Walmsley. Again, Joseph Hume was a principal in this movement. It held a meeting of some five thousand at the Drury Lane Theatre on Monday 13th August 1849. One of the speakers on that day was Feargus O'Connor; after years against, he had come around to the idea of class cooperation. Sir Joshua Walmsley opened proceedings with a courteous 'Gentlemen' although there was a large number of middle and upper-class women there. 'It is honourable to London,' he said, 'that this association has so rapidly developed the necessity of uniting all classes in the attainment of a large, substantial, and permanent measure of reform, that, in the short space of six months, we have succeeded in inspiring confidence where distrust and prejudice formerly existed.'[231] This was met with cheers. Others spoke. Lord Dudley Stuart thought there was no reason why there 'should not be seats in the House of Commons for members elected from the working classes.' More approval. When Feargus O'Connor came forward to add his piece he was met with cheers. He was delighted with the fraternisation between the middle and the working classes, 'the more it was carried out, the greater would be the facilities for removing the obloquy which had been so unjustly attached towards the latter.' O'Connor's views were well received, his change of heart towards the middle-class reformers accepted.

In the closing weeks of 1848, foggy and damp, London's Central Criminal Court had been dealing with the last of the London Chartists involved in August's revolutionary conspiracy and no-one there was concerned with the pros and cons of class cooperation. George Mullins, the twenty-two-year-old surgeon's apprentice, was found guilty on 30th October 1848 of levying war against the Queen and intending to depose her. He was sentenced to life transportation by a judge who called the insurrectionists 'refuse.'[232] James Leach, he who had introduced Julian Harney to Friedrich Engels all those years ago, who had been a delegate in the Chartist Assembly of May and had liaised between the Dublin Confederates and the English Chartists, was sentenced on 10th December at Liverpool's Winter Assizes to a term at Kirkdale prison where Peter McDouall had already spent four months of his two year sentence. And just as these trials were taking place, in the final weeks of 1848, cholera came to London.

At the start of the year everyone had dreaded the coming of the cholera; now, by early October they all knew the infection was heading towards them from the Continent. None knew its cause; it was generally believed to come from putrefaction rising from the ground, creating atmospheric poisoning. Reports of deaths from the cholera in London began to appear in October's papers. By mid-November one hundred and seventy Londoners had died of it, and of the twenty-seven deaths across the river at Bermondsey, Southwark, Newington and Lambeth, sixteen were children. The densely populated working-class areas of London were where the infection spread so easily. It struck the inhabitants of a house in Collingwood Street, Bethnal Green, where eighteen people lived in three rooms. Two children of Mr Tyler a bedstead-maker died, then his wife's mother, upon which the wife, Mrs Tyler, and her remaining four children were removed to Bethnal Green workhouse. Mrs Tyler had recovered from an earlier attack of cholera-like symptoms but she soon died of the real thing in the workhouse along with two more of her children.[233]

And so it went on. St Pancras workhouse sent their children away from the metropolis to an infant pauper asylum out in Tooting, a place called Surrey Hall, run by a Mr Drouet.[234] Mr Drouet had 1,372 children under his care at the time, all sent from thirteen separate workhouses at 4s. 6p. per head per week. Mr Drouet was making a great deal of money from his enterprise. The place was over-crowded and cold. The children's bedding was not sufficient to keep them warm at night. The boys' dormitory had been officially limited to 350 but 500 children slept there, and it was built over a refuse ditch.[235] The cholera reached them at the very end of

December 1848. Within a few days, twenty-five children were dead, more than one hundred ill, and the deaths continued in following days. Children were dying so quickly and in such numbers that the carpenter's shop, where their small bodies were kept, was 'in awful array, in some instances three [bodies] being place in one coffin.'[236] They were still dying two weeks later and more falling ill.

These children and infants were not necessarily orphans. They were paupers and might have entered their respective parish workhouses alone or with a parent; but even with a parent, families were separated under the hated Whig's 1834 New Poor Law so that parents did not always know where or how their child was, and children did not know how their parents fared. There was no escape from this. St Pancras workhouse had some 150 of its own cholera cases to deal with by mid-January, and in all crowded places it was the same story. Such was the state of London in January 1849. But nothing in the public eye compared in dreadfulness to the concentration of deaths at Drouet's asylum. The established system allowed men like Drouet to function as he did. In February he was still running his infants' asylum and 223 children remained under his care.[237]

There were many more middle-class men, respectable mill owners and industrial entrepreneurs doing much the same, making the most of unregulated market opportunities at the expense of child, woman and man. It is reasonable to say that in 1848 middle class entrepreneurs of this stamp represented the majority of their class, yet at the turn of 1849 some, of a reforming spirit, were offering some small hope of a better future to those same children, women and men.

PART THREE

AFTER 1848

15
Death and Deportation: 1849

As 1848 came to an end, London was electrified to hear that Louis Bonaparte had been elected to the French Presidency by a massive majority of the vote. 'Are we to suppose,' wrote the *Morning Chronicle*'s correspondent from Paris on 14th December, 'that France sighs for the revival of the Empire? Or are we to imagine, as the Republicans contend, that the election of Louis Napoleon is a conspiracy on the part of the Legitimist, Orleanists, and Reactionaries of all classes, in conjunction with the [Catholic] Church, for the restoration of the Monarchy.' The *Morning Chronicle*'s correspondent had his finger on the pulse. Within a handful of months of his election, Louis Bonaparte would send troops against Guiseppe Mazzini's newly formed Rome Republic when asked by Pope Pius IX who had been forced from Rome to take refuge down the coast at Gaeta. Louis Napoleon Bonaparte had unilateral control of his country's military and was quite prepared to go to the Pope's aid by way of shoring up his popularity with the French Catholics. As a result, the dreams of Italian liberal Republicanism and French socialism were destroyed. Julian Harney was grief stricken by this act.[238] Within three years, by December 1852, Louis Bonaparte declared himself Napoleon III, Emperor of France, to popular acclaim.

'The revolutionary earthquake which shook thrones to dust, and scattered kings, queens, royal dukes and duchesses, princes and nobles, like sea birds in a storm, has passed away. What are its present results? The old tyrannies restored in almost every country where Liberty achieved a brief and fleeting triumph.' This is Julian Harney writing in November 1849 of the great revolutions of 1848.[239] In Britain, the National Charter Association, though mauled by the Whig administration, did not pass entirely away. As 1849 came in, a new Executive of those who had kept clear of prosecution, Philip McGrath, Samuel Kydd, George Julian Harney and three others, was again meeting in London, at 144 High Holborn, the address of Feargus O'Connor's National Land Company. A feeling of personal failure echoes in Samuel Kydd's comment that the 1848 Executive might have done more during 'an excited time,' yet if they had not done all that they might have done, 'they at least had done all that their means allowed.'[240] The Executive of 1849 would, 'through peaceful and legal means,' continue to work for a universal suffrage, fair electoral districts, payment for MPs and abolition of the property qualification.

Behind all this, the Chartist Victim and Defence Committee, set up to provide for those imprisoned because they had fought for these goals, was floundering. 'We have paid, within the last three months, between £80 and £90 for bail fees,' wrote colleagues from Manchester in December 1848, and 'we shall require £300 within the next three weeks to defend the Chartist victims in the northern district.'[241] In London, solicitors and counsel had been engaged during the critical summer and autumn months of 1848. The solicitor James Macnmara had alone received some £200 in fees. In fact, James Macnmara had done so well that he had, by now, left his grandmother's property at Cleveland Row for a lawyer's chambers at Lincoln's Inn Fields. The cost to the Chartist Defence Committee during the trials was astronomic. Funds were raised through small donations and through the pennies collected from hard-pressed working people in London and the counties. Remember 'Fussell, Shaw, Bezer, Williams, Payne, Cuffay, McDouall etc etc etc,' the Executive Committee pleaded to *Northern Star* readers. 'Remember too...Ernest Jones, Vernon, Lacey, Fay, Looney, Dowling etc etc,' It is the etc etc, which signifies the true situation. For every well-known Chartist and Confederate name, there were dozens unknown.

It had not been many years since London's prisons had indiscriminately incarcerated convicts under their roofs. Classes of prisoner had been introduced over the past twenty years in an attempt to separate the 'simple novice' from the 'artful adept' and the criminal from the prisoner of conscience.[242] By 1849 prisoners to be transported were held at Pentonville, Brixton or Millbank prisons, or in the hulks at Woolwich until their ship sailed. Long and short-term prisoners not to be transported were kept in Houses of Correction or Bridewells.

Ernest Jones, Alexander Sharp, Joseph Williams, John Fussell and Robert Crowe, not to be transported, were imprisoned at Tothill

Bridewell as were a number of those arrested at the Orange Tree on 17th August, one being the young brass turner William Scadding. The leading August conspirators to be transported were kept at one or other of the long-term penal service prisons until the transport ship was ready to sail, which in their case would not be until November 1849. As for James Bezer, the squat, square building of Newgate prison was where he was kept from the time of his arrest in August 1848 until his release in April 1850.

By the autumn of 1849, Ernest Jones had been more than one year at Tothill Bridewell in Westminster. He later recalled being so physically weak by this time that he was incapable of crossing his cell without help. He was disabled with rheumatism and neuralgia and was allowed the comfort of news from his wife Jane and their children only once every three months.[243] Alexander Sharp and Joseph Williams experienced much the same during their time at Tothill, but they did not have to endure it for as long as Ernest Jones.

If you were a prisoner or a workhouse inmate you would be set to pick oakum, that is to unravel old ropes and cords so that their fibres could be reused. It was work of degradation and it shredded your fingers. At Tothill Bridewell was a large hall where some hundreds of men picked oakum at tables each day. The twenty-five-year-old tailor, Chartist and Confederate Robert Crowe, who had publicly defied the London spies at the time of William Smith O'Brien's uprising, was one who joined this number. Each man was supposed to pick a daily two-and-a-half pounds of oakum. Robert Crowe's fingers were so blistered after six weeks of this work that he was unable to fulfil his quota and said he could do it no longer. He was put on bread and water for three days.[244] Ernest Jones, Joseph Williams and Alexander Sharp were also expected to do the same work and at some point also refused. A payment of 5s a week could buy an exemption from the humiliation of oakum picking but there came a time when no shillings were available to the prisoners so, for their refusal, they were punished instead. Strictly speaking, this should not have been happening to the Chartist prisoners. These men were a class of prisoner not sentenced to this regimen but the local magistrates were empowered to insist under a ruling provided by Act 4th George IV, chap 46, sec 38, which effectively overrode the Central Criminal Court's terms of sentence.[245] The prisoners were, then, entirely at the mercy of the prison authorities and local magistrates. This is the issue which had been raised in the House of Commons by Thomas Wakley the year before.

Joseph Williams, like Robert Crowe, was punished for refusing to pick oakum. He was put in solitary confinement for six days on a bread and water diet. This punishment started on 26th August 1849. He had already spent three days under the same terms of punishment in July for secreting letters for another prisoner and during his second period of punishment he became so ill that the prison surgeon allowed him gruel until he recovered; the bread and water routine was then resumed. Prison surgeons knew that a diet of bread and water produces stomach and bowel problems very quickly. Three days after Williams's release from solitary confinement he fell ill again, again with a bowel complaint, and was taken to the prison infirmary. His father visited him there and the son said he had been told he had cholera but that it was not so, it was 'starvation and cold, not cholera.'[246] Joseph Williams, who had earned 16 shillings a week baking bread for his and his family's living, and who had led the great march through the streets of London on the night of 29th May 1848, died on the morning of Friday 7th September 1849.

His death was not the end of it. The family of Alexander Sharp, no longer able to pay the necessary weekly five shillings to keep him from oakum picking, stopped payment in the second week of August. It was Sharp who had stood next to Ernest Jones at Bonner's Field on 4th June 1848 and had told the crowd not to run away from the police, who had said he cared not 'one pin for the police or the military.' He refused the labour of oakum picking and was duly put into solitary confinement and on bread and water. Thereafter, he quickly succumbed to cholera and died a week after Joseph Williams, at 9.30 pm on 14th September 1849.[247] He was twenty-nine years old.

After the deaths of the two Londoners Alexander Sharp and Joseph Williams, a public meeting was held at the Hall of Science, City Road, to look into the causes. This was a process which Thomas Clark, long standing secretary of the National Charter

Association, was glad working people no longer had to face alone: 'the battle had hitherto been fought nearly single-handed; but now fortunately we [have] the middle classes.' Beside him stood the barrister Tindal Atkinson, working on behalf of the two dead men. Here was an example of class cooperation. Sharp's and Williams's deaths, Tindal Atkinson said, had brought him face-to-face for the first time 'with the hard-working and hard-headed operatives.' Now, 'he would use his utmost influence to get them represented, not only by their votes, but in their own persons in the House of Commons.'[248] Some flavour, then, of the broadening shift of attitude. Distinct signs that the representatives of the working classes were open to class cooperation and that the middle classes who hitherto had not ventured behind the pleasant street facades into the filthy courts and allies concealed beyond, were beginning to cast a glance there, if only figuratively. This was just before Henry Mathew's investigative articles appeared in the *Morning Chronicle* and which made it harder still for his middle and upper-class readers to keep their eyes averted from the poor of London.

During these same months, Peter McDouall at Kirkdale prison in Lancashire, whose long fair hair would be cropped by now as hair cropping served as a demoralisation to all prisoners, was by all accounts suffering grievously from depression. His mind was filled with anxiety for his family while he was kept inactive and alone for twenty-three hours out of every twenty-four. Mary Ann McDouall had been offered a house and grocery shop by well-wishers in Liverpool but the business failed; McDouall might have imagined the surreal possibility of his family ending up in a workhouse. During a short imprisonment at Kirkdale the Irish woolcomber and Chartist, George White, had managed to speak with him during their day's hour of exercise. McDouall was patently worried about his family, was wearing prison garb and was engaged in degrading work. White felt it unlikely that his fellow prisoner would survive his two years' imprisonment.[249] An effort was made to get McDouall an early release. His legal representative, W.R. Roberts, tried for some months to secure a Writ of Error against his sentence but the whole of the funds necessary for this were never raised. McDouall's despair deepened. Mary Ann, visiting him in May

1849, saw that his health was failing while he asked that whatever money had been raised (some £10) should be given to her and their four children, one a new-born.

The London solicitor, James Macnmara, who by the latter half of 1849 had given up hope of receiving his outstanding fees which amounted to more than £100, sued Feargus O'Connor for the money at the Queen's Bench, using the letter written by O'Connor the year before as proof of liability. O'Connor no longer enjoyed the income from sales of the *Northern Star* that once he had. Its numbers had declined since the Kennington Common disappointment. Macnmara won his case against his erstwhile mentor but was vilified by some of O'Connor's colleagues. He quit his chambers at 58 Lincoln's Inn Fields, went to live at Tranmere in Cheshire, styled himself 'a gentleman' and began a family.

Only in Ireland was there still a spark of activity. In September 1849 another rebellion against England was tried, this time led by James Fintan Lalor. Lalor suffered severe physical disabilities. He was 'deaf, near-sighted, ungainly, and deformed,' said one who knew him, 'and his deficiencies cut him off not only from any career needing sympathy and publicity, but even from social intercourse except with his nearest kin.'[250] But Lalor was the inspiration behind John Mitchel's 1847 plan of civil disobedience. His was the mind behind much of what had happened in Ireland, hence London, in 1848. He was, said journalist Charles Gavan Duffy, 'a genuine revolutionary force.'[251]

Lalor's rebels, led by Joseph Brenan and wearing white sash and belt, were scattered at Cappoquin on 16th September 1849 when caught between police and men firing from the property of Sir Richard Keane.[252] The Westminster Parliament was in recess at the time. News of the attempt appeared briefly in the London presses; the provincial papers seemed more interested. Again, some of the rebels, Brenan included, fled to America while at home the potato blight and famine continued.

John Bright visited Ireland in 1849. Here was enough 'to horrify the stoutest, and to move the hardest heart. Ruined cottages, uncultivated lands, crowded workhouses, fever, cholera, famine, scores of victims buried in trenches...The story is frightful, and I will not write the details.'[253]

Earlier, in June 1849, a notice from London that the death sentences passed on William Smith O'Brien, Terence Bellew McManus, Thomas Meagher and Patrick O'Donoghue were commuted to life transportation reached the governor of Dublin's Richmond Bridewell where the prisoners had been held since their trial at Clonmel. There had been some legal difficulty attaching to this commutation but London's politicians had got around it through the Transportation for Treason Act, passed expressly to avoid turning the leading Confederates into martyrs and for the purpose of sending them as far from Britain as possible. This did not suit William Smith O'Brien who tried very hard, through legal means, to avoid transportation but transported he was. The war sloop *Swift* arrived at Kingstown, now Dun Laoghaire, on Sunday 8th July 1849 and the next morning sailed away to the other side of the world, taking the Irish Confederate leaders with her.[254]

Seven weeks after the sailing of the *Swift*, the London transportees: sixty-one-year-old William Cuffay (returned to London after a transfer to Wakefield's Convict Prison), Joseph Richie who had been responsible for making the fire bombs in August 1848, and the very much younger Thomas Fay and George Mullins, all were put on the *Adelaide* at Woolwich. The Chartist-Confederates William Lacey and William Dowling went aboard with them. The *Adelaide*'s holds had been thoroughly cleaned in order to keep her total cargo of three hundred prisoners as infection-free as possible during the three months' journey ahead. She sailed on 17th August 1849, stopped off at Portsmouth, Cowes and Portland to pick up her full complement of transportees, then set out to open sea. There were others on board connected with the 1848 trials for sedition though the majority were convicted of theft or burglary. One man was transported for murder. This was Joseph Constantine, a Chartist who had been at Ashton-under-Lyne when Peter McDouall delivered the speech which sent him to Kirkdale prison in 1848. Constantine almost certainly was not guilty of murder, but it had been a policeman killed and the young Constantine was dispatched on the *Adelaide* just the same.[255]

Also sailing on the *Adelaide* were thirty children, all boys. They had been picked up at Cowes from Parkhurst prison. Some were as young as twelve. Transportation of Parkhurst's children had been going on for seven years and would continue for three more after the *Adelaide*'s sailing. In that time nearly two thousand children and youths from Parkhurst were sent from England to Australia to be put out for apprenticeship on arrival. They were considered the lucky ones. Their counterparts (boys and girls) kept at Millbank or Pentonville in London were not chosen for rehabilitation as the boys sent to Parkhurst were and their stories remain obscure. Transportation of undesirables, child and adult, was attractive and logical to British governments, while the encouragement by successive governments of voluntary emigration to Australia and Canada meant the loss of a great many of Britain's most determined and hopeful to other lands.

16
Class Cooperation

Ernest Jones did not die in Westminster's Tothill Bridewell although there were times when he thought he would. He was released on 9th July 1850 and came out 'red as fire' and though physically wrecked was in all other respects ready, vigorously, to spurn any cooperation with the middle classes.[256] His release from prison was greeted with immense jubilation, especially by the people of Halifax in Yorkshire. There were three musical bands, a carriage drawn by four greys, an evening's entertainments; and to the celebrating working people, with Julian Harney at his side, the exhausted Ernest Jones vowed to continue to fight for the Charter.

But rapprochement between the working and the middle classes went forward even so. Some began not to care how reform came, as long as it came. At the start of the 1850s Lord Palmerston spoke of each man 'constantly striving to raise himself in the social scale,' and at their end Samuel Smiles was writing about 'Self-Help' through which this raising might be achieved. [257] And to one working man visiting from Ireland, London was the physical manifestation of these allurements: 'the beauty and riches of the shops of London surpasses all the world, it is all a stream of gass [sic] light...the streets are beautiful and wide, the footpaths twice as wide as in Ireland...I was greatly amazed.'[258] But for more than one million of London's people living in the back streets, alleys and courts lying behind those streams of gas light, nothing changed. Londoners continued to die, barely clothed, unfed, in unfurnished and unheated rooms and on London's streets. Children were found dying of want; men sold their shoes for food; a seventy-three-year-old woman called Agnes Edgell died of cold at her street stall; families of six, seven, eight, lived and slept together in single rooms 4 meters by 3 meters. All these, and many more tales from the foothills of hell were publicised in 1860 and 1861 in London's *Morning Post* by John Hollingshead.[259] The stories of Londoners' private sufferings mirrored those of Ireland's cottiers during their years of famine. The majority of these people were quite beyond any sort of self-help. There were a few, like James Bezer, who managed to create something for themselves but for most it was just a case of survival until even that was beyond them.

For Julian Harney, this was the result of a system of accumulation and greed which viewed and used needy people as 'hands' and those not fit to be hands as irredeemably useless. He would not be one to look to the middle classes for succour, the 'bourgeoisie' benefitting from this system; they would remain the adversary to him. '*From the ranks of the Proletarians* must come the saviours of industry,' he wrote for the *Northern Star* in November 1849.

It was now that the man who had been Harney's mentor years earlier and who had walked away from the entire goings-on of 1848, returned to the scene. James Bronterre O'Brien – no relation to William Smith O'Brien but a fellow Irishman – had until recently lived in retreat from London with his wife Sophia O'Brien and their children in Douglas on the Isle of Man. A seminal figure in the social reform movement of the 1830s and 40s, he had mentored Julian Harney in those early years. It is said he was one who informed much of Friedrich Engels' and Karl Marx's philosophy.[260] Bronterre O'Brien was a man of great tragedy. A drinker, sensitive, a tall stooping figure who was unable to best the behemoth that was Feargus O'Connor and who ran rough-shod over him: 'In pursuance of his general policy of driving every man out of the movement that he could not make a Connorman of, or whose influence he thought stood in the way of his making the Chartist Body a mere mob, [. . . he] fell foul of me and of all my political and personal friends throughout the country who took a part in public affairs.'[261] With O'Connor now in decline, Bronterre O'Brien returned to Chartist activity. And another, the thirty-two-year-old George Jacob Holyoake who had been a socialist for a decade (in the sense of Owenite cooperative, communitarian and anti-religious socialism) and who famously had been imprisoned for blasphemy in 1842, began to associate with the Chartists. The connection, as was so often the case in these things, was Julian Harney. Harney had known Holyoake when both men lived in Sheffield in the early 1840s. They had long been good friends. The relationship between Bronterre O'Brien and Harney went back even further.

Bronterre O'Brien established an organisation in November 1849 which he called The National Reform League. Meetings were held at 72 Newman Street, off Oxford Street, where socialism was expounded in an advanced form. For two decades O'Brien had been formulating his doctrines. Nationalise the land, create tenancies for the people and the prime cause of society's ills, private land ownership, would be dealt with. Nationalise railroads, canals, docks, fisheries, mines, gas and water, so that these assets might be let out and the rental income used for public services. No future universal suffrage parliament would allow these national utilities to fall into the hands of private speculators 'unless it were stark mad,' he wrote.[262] And a symbolic currency 'exactly expressive of the labour-content of each article or commodity' was put forward as a fair economic system.[263] Julian Harney, still O'Connor's editor, reported in the *Northern Star* on the meetings of Bronterre O'Brien's National Reform League, also on his own Fraternal Democrats and on continental politics. He was feeling like 'a "pioneer", the teacher of "strange doctrines", the proclaimer of principles which startle the many, and are but timidly acknowledged even by the few.'[264]

And so Chartism, the movement which had openly joined with the Irish Confederacy in March 1848, then had gone on to produce a clandestine movement for revolution in the spring and summer months, began its slow demise as it became a thing of different parts and suffered the disagreements of its leading members. There were those like Thomas Clark and Feargus O'Connor who welcomed middle class cooperation. Bronterre O'Brien also was open to it: there were 'good and wise' men in the middle classes whose 'love of justice raise them above class prejudices.'[265] Yet there were many others, those like Julian Harney and Ernest Jones, who saw class cooperation as the equivalent to hugging a viper to one's breast. Harney persisted in his hope for the rise of international socialist-democracy and had no time for the 'bourgeoisie' irrevocably driven by financial profit. But howsoever he and Jones might view it, reform did evolve into a process which incorporated middle class efforts.

It was as if 1848 had expended the last of the hope and energy of the body of Chartists so that thereafter the great mass of active working people was not there in the same spirit. The class cooperation of the following years might be viewed as a process of absorption of the working classes by the middle classes into the establishment: John Foster in his foreword to Mick Jenkin's *The General Strike of 1842* describes this as a process that 'demanded that organized labour operate on the terms set by the capitalist state, and rigidly separate the 'economic' and the 'political' spheres of its activity.'[266] On the other hand, in 1963 Edward Thompson wrote that the workers: 'having failed to overthrow capitalist society proceed to warren of it end-to-end.'[267] Howsoever it was, the early processes of class cooperation did, eventually, include even Ernest Jones' support. Extension of voting rights, not a universal franchise at one sweep, was the way in which reform would slowly proceed.

In 1866 John Russell, again prime minister, thought it time for another Reform Bill. A deputation from the middle-class National Reform Union, accompanied by working men, travelled to London in February 1866 to lobby Russell. A partial, or reasonable share in voting rights based on property ownership was accepted at this time.[268] However, it was not until an open-air meeting of the working class Reform League (formed in 1865 and not to be confused with Bronterre O'Brien's National Reform League) was refused admittance into London's Hyde Park in July 1866 that the impetus for reform really took off. Three days of violent demonstrations was the result of the authorities' Hyde Park prohibition. Middle-class mill-owner John Bright was finally propelled into leadership of the reform campaign, and in the August of 1867 a Tory government, under Lord Derby, brought in a Second Reform Act which almost doubled the electorate.[269]

With the one exception of annual parliaments, the terms of the 1848 People's Charter were won in incremental steps over the next seventy years. Abolition of the property qualification for members of parliament: enacted in 1858. Voting rights: extended in 1867. Vote by ballot: gained in 1872 (whereby employers could no longer coerce staff, tenant or worker to vote their way). Voting rights:

extended again in 1884. And in 1911 payment of MPs was brought in by a Liberal government.

It took a world war before a universal male franchise, the fundamental principle of the People's Charter, received Royal Assent on 6th February 1918. In 1848 the fight for these constitutional changes had brought hundreds of thousands of working people into conflict with the authorities and sent many of them into prison, exile or into their graves. Women, whose great-grandmothers had fought for these principles, had to wait for equivalent voting rights until 1928.

And so, it could be said that the People's Charter was won but the great social change which many had thought would be gained by the implementation of its terms was not won. Extreme poverty and social handicap were not ended by it; it was Bronterre O'Brien who, in 1841, said of gaining the universal vote: 'All the real work will then remain to be done.'[270]

17
Ireland: 'That coming storm'

Socialism was not what the Irish Confederates had had on their minds in 1848. Their campaign had been in the cause of nationalism: to free Ireland from English control. In 1849 the Confederate leaders found themselves exiled to the far side of the world by a British government which tenaciously held on to Ireland but which abdicated responsibility for its people.

John Mitchel's journey to Van Diemen's Land took nearly two years. His first stop in 1848 was the penal colony of Bermuda, then a tortuous journey via the Cape of Good Hope to Van Diemen's Land, so he did not arrive there until April 1850, six months after the exiled Confederate leaders had reached there from Ireland. On their three months' journey William Smith O'Brien, Terence Bellew McManus, Thomas Meagher and Patrick O'Donoghue had filled their time with copious reading, often aloud to one another, and after passing the Cape Verde Islands, Patrick O'Donoghue, according to his diary, threw away his dirty old wig as his hair had grown, 'like that of the strong Nazarite, Samson...though I am now in the hands of the Philistines.'[271] There would be no acceptance by the exiled Confederates of their fates at the hands of the English Philistines after their arrival at Hobart on 29th October 1849, especially when it became clear to them that their sacrifice did not inspire renewed efforts at home. Beyond the Fintan Lalor attempt which took place while they were aboard the *Swift*, Ireland remained relatively quiet for some time. Once settled at the other side of the world they started planning their escapes.

John Mitchel was joined in Van Diemen's Land by his wife Jane and their children. The family lived at Bothwell under parole from the authorities on a farm of over two hundred acres, 'not large,' according to Jane Michel but she thought Van Diemen's Land a beautiful country. 'The house', she wrote to her friend Mary Thompson of O'Meath, 'is built on a knoll, and around it is a lawn of 100 acres pasture, through a portion of it runs the river Clyde; skirting it are fine forests of trees, and behind them rise the noble mountains covered with bush.' 'The children are in perfect health, and enjoy this sort of life beyond everything.'[272] Their servants, who were convicts, slept in a wooden hut. They are 'sad plagues,' she wrote, 'and the women far worse than the men. I have a Tipperary woman who was convicted at Clonmel at the time of O'Brien's trial...My cook is a man.'

William Smith O'Brien's time in exile was harder than that of his friends. '[H]e who was so erect, is getting quite a stoop,' Jane Mitchel wrote. O'Brien would not live on parole: it required a promise not to attempt escape which he could not give as he intended it, and even tried it unsuccessfully. And so, for the first fourteen months of his time at the penal colony he lived as a prisoner under the authority of the Governor. He would not have his family join him from Ireland because of the humiliation to them. Withholding himself from the comforts of his family and from the benefits of life on parole made his time there wretched. What he must have felt when he took a position as tutor to a doctor's children is open to conjecture. Smith O'Brien remained in Van Diemen's Land until 1854 when he was released on the condition that he would not return to Ireland. But he did return to Ireland in July 1856 after receiving an unconditional pardon from the British Crown.

The others escaped: Terence Bellew McManus in 1850, Thomas Meagher in 1852 having married Catherine Bennett the daughter of a free settler.[273] After reaching California, McManus stayed in Los Angeles while Thomas and Catherine Meagher, who were about to become parents, went on to New York. John and Jane Mitchel took their turn in 1853. While escaping, John Mitchel spent some weeks as a fugitive on the island until he managed to board the same ship as that boarded by his wife and children – the British brig *Emma* bound for California. The Mitchels disembarked at Los Angeles and they, like the Meaghers, travelled across the continent to New York.

It took a full ten years after the 1848 rising but by 1858 all was in place for the founding of the Fenian Brotherhood. John O'Mahony and Michael Doheny, both of who had made their escapes from Ireland to Paris and freedom, were by now also in New York. As to James Stephens, he too had escaped to Paris but did not immediately follow the others to New York. He was back in Ireland by 1857. Stephens was one of those who had pulled William Smith O'Brien to safety during the battle at Boulagh Commons on 29th July 1848. For his pains he had ended up in a ditch and, known to be injured, had escaped capture by the British authorities by faking his own death and staging his own funeral. With O'Mahony and Doheny in New York and Stephens now back in Ireland, the Fenian societies in both countries were formed. Stephens was far more likely a leader of revolutionary men than Smith O'Brien. There was something of the megalomaniac in his personality. He was known to be as high-handed and opinionated as Smith O'Brien was honourable and gentlemanly. In Ireland Stephens established the Irish Republican Brotherhood, formed as a secret society intended to make the country an independent republic. London's politicians, it was claimed, and rightly as it turns out, 'would never concede self-government to the force of argument, but only to the argument of force.'[274]

In London in 1867, this being the year of the second Reform Act which enfranchised a percentage of those who had demanded it in 1848, the deadly ire of the Fenians was felt for the first time. In an attempt to free Burke and Casey, two of their men imprisoned in London's Clerkenwell House of Correction, a cask of gunpowder was set and exploded against the twenty-five feet high prison wall facing Corporation Lane. This was done late on the afternoon of 13th December 1867, just after the local dairyman, who later would give evidence, had done his rounds. It was a massive explosion which brought down not just sixty feet of prison wall but also a great many of the terraced houses on the north side of the lane. It did not free Burke or Casey but it did kill forty of the people living on Corporation Lane and injured many more, there and on Upper Woodbridge Street. 'When the explosion took place I was indoors,' said one from Upper Woodbridge Street, 'and lifted off my feet, and thrown to the ground senseless, and knew no more till I was brought to in a house on the opposite side of the street where I had been carried, by hearing someone say 'Her house is on fire.'[275]

The dead and wounded, wrote *The Times*, have 'suffered in a public cause, they are the victims of a conspiracy which, under the names of patriotism and liberty, has declared war on the

Government and society of these islands.'[276] Children were killed and many injured that late afternoon. Some premature births were brought about by physical trauma. Those who survived the explosion were taken to St Bartholomew's Hospital, some to the Royal Free Hospital on Grey's Inn Road. A small colony of watchmakers on Corporation Lane lost their tools, and washerwomen and manglewomen lost their equipment. But the loss of their homes troubled most. One of the hospitals' doctors was impressed by the anxiety this produced in his patients. Clerkenwell parish church's incumbent, Robert Maguire, called it 'the thorough state of dislocation of everything.'[277]

In Gladstone's lament at the outset of the famine of the 1840s: 'Ireland! Ireland! That cloud in the west, that coming storm,' there resounded the five years of famine to come, the revolutionary attempts of 1848 in Ireland, London and the rest of Britain, the misery of countless migrations, transportations and imprisonments, the deaths of people like those on Corporation Lane, and all the troubles of future generations.

18
The Prisoners' Fates

The lives of the men of 1848 were profoundly dislocated after their revolutionary attempts, and so were their families'. Peter McDouall was released from Kirkdale prison in June 1850; just weeks after the death of his ten-year-old daughter. This was the very thing he had so dreaded. After losing their child, Mary Ann McDouall wrote to the Home Secretary George Grey upon which her husband's release was brought forward by six weeks but not before the magistrates overseeing Kirkdale prison placed a bail of two years as a condition; a condition over-ruled by Grey. The government 'were not desirous of detaining me in prison!' McDouall wrote.[278] He came from Kirkdale a self-declared class co-operator. And although not intending to 'bury' himself, 'I do not intend to attach myself to any party.' He attempted to run a publication from Manchester and to re-establish his medical practice at Ashton-under-Lyne: effectively a return to his early-Chartist days. Neither enterprise succeeded so he and Mary Ann did what so many were doing, they emigrated to Australia in 1853 and within a year the fiery, personable Peter Murray McDouall, with such a mind for organisation, was dead. He was not yet forty. Mary Ann McDouall managed to get back to England with her children and settled in Nottingham to run a newsagency on Lower Parliament Street. Living with her in 1861 was her son James a sawyer, Grace a hosier, Mary Ann a box maker, and Sophia Jane a scholar.[279]

Feargus O'Connor did not find himself imprisoned in 1848 but he had spent seventeen months in York prison between 1840 and 1841 so knew something about it. The year 1851 was the year in which his physical and mental decline began to show. Because of an untreated syphilitic disease working its way through his body and brain, his behaviour grew irrational and by 1852 had reached the bizarre. In February 1852 he went alone to see George Henry Lewes' *The Game of Speculation* playing at the Lyceum Theatre off the Strand and as the orchestra began playing the evening's overture, the tall and now cadaverous-looking Irishman, from a seat in the second row of the dress circle, began a noisy and animated imitation of the instruments. He jigged up and down, waved his arms like a violin player, boo-booed like a drum and, when asked, refused to stop. He slapped the policeman who tried to remove him from his seat, was arrested and spent some days in Clerkenwell's House of Correction in great distress and humiliation. Knowing that total decline was ahead of him, he managed to flee to New York where he caused embarrassment and, after two weeks, took the long journey on a steamer back to England. His friend G.W.M. Reynolds took him to his home for a short while before a place was found for him at the Manor House Asylum in Chiswick where he seems to have been comfortable. After much controversy between those of his old colleagues who sought his comfort and his sister Harriet who appears to have been more concerned with her own, he was suddenly and forcibly removed from the asylum by her to die two weeks later, on 30th August 1855 in her house at Notting Hill. These were two weeks of dire distress. He had been a man both greatly loved and fiercely disliked; one who, it was said at his grave side, few had understood.[280] The outcomes of the continental revolutions of 1848 would have been of no great surprise to him. The change of ministry in France in February 1848 amounted to nothing more than 'a transfer of power from glutted to needy officials,' and he opposed the revolutionary action in England during the tumultuous spring and summer months of that year.[281]   And so there passed an outstanding man.

Ernest Jones headed the Chartist movement after Feargus O'Connor's decline in 1852 but by then Chartism was not the movement it had been. The issue of class cooperation began to overshadow earlier principles and to divide leading personalities. What is more, the revolutionary fire of the working people had gone out and everyone was focused on getting on with things as they were – social aspiration not socialism seemed to be the thing. Yet for three of the primary leaders of the 1848 movement the foundational principle remained; each had one thing in common, each had experienced a revelation which changed their lives. Feargus O'Connor's eyes had been opened to the dreadfulness of the effects of middle class accumulation early one morning in Manchester in 1835 when he had seen the mill workers with their pallid faces going to their workplace, their 'earthly hell'; Peter McDouall had witnessed things at the mills and factories of Lancashire which never left him; Ernest Jones experienced a profound awakening when he read of the state of the industrial operatives from the pages of the *Northern Star* in 1846. It is this which drove them: the dreadful condition of the working people. The People's Charter was supposed to be the answer, its fundamental aim to elect to parliament Chartist sympathisers through a universal vote. Two years after his release from prison Ernest Jones stood as a parliamentary candidate for Halifax.

Jones had tried at Halifax in 1847 when it had been innovative for a Chartist to seek a parliamentary seat and he had received a surprisingly high proportion of the votes against the standing Whig and Tory. His second attempt in 1852 was far less successful. In 1857, the year that Jane Jones died, he tried for a seat at Manchester and, having gone through great sea-changes in his public and private life, the very next year he founded the Manhood Suffrage movement in London which embraced class cooperation. Ernest Jones had drastically revised his principles; he now sought a middle-class alliance with what remained of the Chartist movement.[282] His revision of principle on this matter shocked many and did not help him when he stood as a parliamentary candidate for Nottingham the following year, 1859. In 1868 he again tried at Manchester. This was one year after the passing of the second Reform Act and, with the support of those city workers who had a vote to cast for the first time, his share of the poll resurged. But it was Liberals Thomas Bazley and Jacob Bright and the Tory Hugh Birley who won the three available seats. Until his dying day, Ernest Jones never gave up trying to gain a parliamentary seat.

'I am convinced there are thirty years of health and life in me,' he had said at the time of his release from Tothill prison in 1850.[283] Had he not been drenched with rain one winter's evening at Manchester eighteen years later and been too long in his suit of wet clothing, his prediction might have come true; he might have gone to the Houses of Parliament not as a petitioner but as a member with some influence. But the wet clothing brought illness which sent him to his bed just as he was contesting the 1869 ballot following a challenge against Hugh Birley. He died on 26th January 1869. One hundred thousand people came out on to the streets of Manchester for his funeral.

As to the conspirators of August 1848: William Cuffay was not immediately joined by his wife Mary after his transportation to Van Diemen's Land. Mary went to live with her sister-in-law at Chatham and worked as a nurse until the money was found for a passage for her on the *Panama* which sailed on 27th April 1853 with nearly four hundred emigrants on board. And so, after five years apart William and Mary Cuffay were reunited and lived together at Hobart for another seventeen years. William Cuffay received a pardon in 1857 and continued his political activities in Hobart until he died at the local workhouse's Brickfields Invalid Depot on 29th July 1870. He was eighty-two years old. Mary had died the year before.

William Dowling, one of the London Confederates who had been imprisoned at Newgate and then transported with William Cuffay on the convict ship *Adelaide*, resumed his art as a painter after arriving in Van Diemen's Land. His Irish-born fiancée sailed out to join him and together they enjoyed Dowling's success as a portrait photographer and painter in studios at Hobart and Launceston. He died at Launceston on 3rd August 1877. George Mullins, he who had pointed to the gas flame at the Lord Denham on the eve of the planned rising of August 1848, made his way to Maitland Australia after his transportation on the *Adelaid* where, it is said, he was joined by his father. Mullins worked as a medical practitioner and died on 8th April 1863 at the hospital where he practised.[284]

As to the Irish Confederates: Patrick O'Donoghue who had been born in poor circumstances in Ireland, died in no better circumstances in New York in 1854. Thomas Meagher having escaped from Van Diemen's Land in 1852 joined a company of New York Irish to fight with Union forces in the American Civil War, then formed the Irish Brigade. After the civil war and having taken-up American citizenship, Meagher became governor of Montana and is said to have led some action against the Native Americans.

He was to drown in the Missouri River in 1867, an event which raised conspiracy theories for the next fifty years. Two statues stand in his memory, one in Helena Montana, one in Waterford Ireland.

Terence Bellew McManus, who made it to America from Van Diemen's Land in 1850, died in California in the January of 1861. It was felt by those who knew him in California that he should be reburied in Irish soil. There was some resistance to this idea from James Stephens, by then back in Ireland, who feared that a burial in Ireland of one of the 1848 rebels might precipitate a revolution before he was ready to lead one. Nevertheless, the arrival of McManus's body from America was expected in Ireland during the whole of October 1861 until finally it did arrive on the 30th, at Cork, on the Inman Line's steamer *City of Washington*, and from there taken to Dublin where it lay in the Hall of the Mechanics' Institute until burial on 11th November. Monday, 11th November turned out to be a wet and gloomy day for so symbolic an event as the funeral of one of the leading Confederate rebels of 1848. Historian Leon Ó Broin considers it to have been 'a turning point in Irish history.'[285]

'The head of the procession has now reached the corner of Britain-street,' wrote an eye witness as Terence Bellew McManus's coffin progressed through Dublin's streets, '...we look back. The scene before us is truly grand and imposing...the vast space from Mountjoy-square, away back to the Custom house on the quays, is one mass of human beings – all animated as if by one mind...to show to the world how Irishmen esteem an Irish patriot.'[286] The priest Patrick Lavelle felt the independence of Ireland to be fore-figured as he stood at McManus's grave side in Glasnevin Cemetery that day.

Another Confederate whose coffin was followed through the streets of Dublin by thousands was William Smith O'Brien. He died at sixty, on 16th June 1864 at Bangor in Wales. He had been eight years in Ireland following his pardon but left again in an attempt to improve his health. It is an irony that he did not breathe his last on home soil. A statue of him stands on O'Connell Street Dublin, arms folded, in his prime, statesman and patriot. In his memoir Thomas Meagher spoke of Smith O'Brien thus: 'to advance and face the murderous fire where no such encouragements are seen or heard, but where everything is downcast and driftless, and the disciplined power of a masterly Government confronts you, whilst a mere handful of men, miserably armed, and still more miserably trained, is all that backs you – this is an exceptional courage of a rare order and occurrence.'[287] An heroic figure then. A man who knowingly sacrificed his reputation and his life for a cause in which he believed.

The London Confederate, Robert Crowe, who spent two years in Tothill Bridewell because of a defiant speech given in 1848, would have been disappointed in his hero John Mitchel had he known the whole of it. Robert Crowe had first seen London in 1837 as a boy when he sailed there from Dublin; he was still there in the aftermath of the failed continental risings, when London was taking in refugees from Italy, France, Austria, Hungary, Poland. Then, in the winter of 1854 he decided on voluntary emigration; he boarded the *Andrew Foster* and sailed to New York. The memoirs he completed in 1901 give no indication that he had any idea during his time working as a tailor in Georgia, probably just before the American Civil War, that John Mitchel was also in the south expounding on the virtues of slavery in America. Robert Crowe was very nearly tarred and feathered, perhaps worse, by the inhabitants of Athens Georgia when they heard he held abolitionist views; had he known of Mitchel's support of and campaign for slavery in America, his disappointment in the man he had admired and whose cause he had taken up and been imprisoned for in 1848 would have gone deep. Robert Crowe never returned to England as far as it is known. John Mitchel sailed back to Ireland early in 1875 to contest a seat in the British parliament for Tipperary but only a few weeks after his arrival he died at Newry on Saturday 20th March.

As to the Chartist Londoner James Bezer, he was released from Newgate prison in April 1850 and a few days later his appearance at a South London Chartist meeting was greeted with great cheering. With East End spark he told his audience that the Whigs had been 'very very kind' to him although his time in Newgate had not reformed him. He had gone to prison thinking his principles were right; now he was 'sure they were.' The hall rang with laughter. They all knew he was a seller of fish? Well, his accusers at the

Central Criminal Court had said he 'offered to sell Lord John Russell a pike – a pike, yes gentlemen a pike. (Roars of laughter.) Ah, it was easy for them to laugh, but allow him to say it put all the old ladies in court into a state of *"Terroris extremis"*.' He, Bezer, was not a learned man 'but he had searched Johnson, Entick and others, and had there found that a pike is a fish, and of course by a parity of reason, a fish is a pike. (Laughter.)' As a merchant of fish, he would like to have had the 'patronage of the First Minister of the Crown, but instead of giving him an order for the pike, he had given him an order for the 'Stone Jug!' (Laughter and applause)[288]

A native exponent of Cockney wit, James Bezer told another audience (for he went on a speaking tour after his release from prison) that prisoners' classifications were a chimera, that it was more to do with 'the weight of their pockets.'[289] He was funny and flippant yet his time in Newgate had been bad. He and his Chartist companion, John Shaw, National Assembly delegate for Tower Hamlets, had been confined in two of Newgate's cells for twelve months, 'until rheumatism and illness laid them both on their backs.' Shaw had ended up on crutches for a while. Yet he, Bezer, emerged from Newgate still a Chartist and now a Republican. The street selling was replaced with writing and the selling of radical books at 183 Fleet Street (famed printing office of Richard Carlile) and he was to be an influential figure within the National Charter Association over the next two years. His memoir shows him to be, boy and man, resistant to the control of those with power over him – workhouse guardians, dispensers of charity, church ministers – and able to see clear through the conceit. He bristled at charity's condescensions and objected to church attitudes but, unlike George Jacob Holyoake who engaged in public battle with the church, James Bezer had a dissenter's soft-spot for it (especially his childhood Sunday school on Raven Row) and largely treated the topic at arm's length and with critical good-humour. His attitude to life seems to have come with a good deal of comic irony and nerveless pragmatism which, to survive life in East End London, were essential characteristics. For the entirety of his London years he and his family moved every few months from one rent to another, as did vast numbers of London's population. In 1848 one of his and Jane's addresses was 2 Shepherd and Flock Court, off two alleys behind Colman Street, another was 3 Sherrold's Buildings, Bishopsgate; in 1850 the family was living at 32 Bartholomew Close, Smithfields, then at 6 Sycamore Street, Old Street; and so it went on. In 1852 they were at 10 Milford Lane, the Strand, where he and Jane lost another child, their baby John James.

Bezer was by now in his mid-thirties and acting as publisher of the *Star of Freedom*, the renamed *Northern Star* still printing at the premises at 16 Great Windmill Street. To avoid debt, he advised his selling agents that the *Star of Freedom* would conduct business only through ready money. Agents would receive no credit and must make '*immediate payment*'.[290] All money orders were made out payable to him through the Strand Post Office. Julian Harney was still the paper's editor and would take over its publishing at the end.

At this time, Julian Harney, now living at 4, Brunswick Row, Bloomsbury, was exercised over the welfare of the refugees coming into London after the failed continental revolutions. He felt it to be a sacred duty to help them and he began fund raising on their behalf. Some who subscribed to the fund were Giuseppe Mazzini (back in London after his defeat at Louis Bonaparte's hands), G.W.M. Reynolds, J.M. Ludlow a Christian Socialist and acquaintance of Bezer, and Viscount Godrich. It is now that something untoward took place between James Bezer and monies coming in to the *Star of Freedom*. A cheque from Viscount Godrich was missed. Julian Harney made enquiries while Bezer, according to his biographer David Shaw, disappeared from London on a ship bound for Australia. Alone.[291] Jane Bezer and surviving children were left behind in London; theirs was a relationship which James, very likely Jane too, had rued from the start. James Bezer had moved on from the years of his East End childhood when he and his mother had survived on parish charity and pennies from a daily twelve hours of work and it seems that nothing would keep him from moving on again to a life he imagined more promising. James Bezer was a London survivor.

His biographer finds that Bezer changed his name to John Bezer Drew (Drew being his mother's family name) in time for his marriage to Elizabeth Roberts at Christchurch, Geelong, Victoria,

Australia on 11th May 1854. It did not seem to matter that Jane Bezer lived on in London and would give birth to at least one more child. He reverted to a life of ever-changing occupations: a shoemaker, a newsagent, a fruit vendor, a postman, a journalist for the *Ararat Advertiser*, a hawker, a general trader; and he involved himself in the politics of Melbourne. He told an audience at Melbourne's Eastern Market in 1875 that the landowners and monopolists of the colony were taking care of their own interests 'to the injury of the masses.' It was time for older men like himself, 'who knew the poverty that existed in England among millions of people through the monopoly of a few, to say to the young men of this colony: "Wake up! or the abuses of the old country will come on you!"'[292] At the close of December 1887 he had a stroke, the effects of which he survived for two weeks. James Bezer died, forty years after the revolutions of 1848 and after half a life time spent in pioneer Australia, on 12th January 1888 at Moray Place, South Melbourne. During his seventy-one years he had buried six of his children. His last occupation, out of the plethora he had had, was bill-poster.

19
Why No Revolution in Britain?

Feargus O'Connor believed that the threat of a combined force of Chartist and Irish Confederate would shake an obtuse parliament. The idea was sound in principle: co-timed Irish and Chartist uprisings might well have been too much for establishment forces to handle but O'Connor was mistaken in hoping that the threat would be enough to persuade parliament to rethink its views on reform. His adversaries knew exactly the man they were dealing with: that he would never lead a revolt. Instead of softening, the authorities hardened and out-manoeuvred the protestors at every turn and then relied on the courts to dispose of them. Besides which, the Chartists and the Confederates were so very different in purpose that no combined leadership existed. Even at street level, Dorothy Thompson writing in 1989 explored the possibility that the militant Irish in mainland Britain might have inhibited action in the traditionally strong Chartist areas of South Wales, Leicester, Nottingham and Birmingham: that the cultures did not meld well.[293] It also is possible that the Chartists there and elsewhere resented being the ones to keep army troops busy in their own streets in order to keep them from the streets of Ireland. Also the influence of non-conformist churches on members of the working classes probably played a restraining hand. Even so, it is safe to say that in London the Confederate clubs and the Chartist groups worked closely together.

The consensus among historians of Chartism is that the movement was a constitutional, never a truly insurrectionary one. The events of 1848, though, show that genuine insurrectionary elements stirred behind the party's public face and came to the fore at this likely time. After Kennington Common, Chartism can fairly be described as insurrectionary. Many rank and file Chartists would have been affected by their rebellious Confederate neighbours living across the landing or up the stairs and with whom, politically, they had long been in sympathy and were now officially allied thanks to the efforts of O'Connor. And the presence of disaffected continental émigrés in London had had its effect. For year upon year, the

Chartists and the Irish Repealers had striven to have their voices heard. In the eight weeks running up to Kennington their continental counterparts had, with demonstrable effect, acted unilaterally, and there were some leading Chartists who appear to have been willing to risk the same on the day of the Kennington Common meeting of 10th April 1848, had fate allowed. They knew the Charter would be rejected by parliament. The letter written by Thomas Allsop, O'Connor's close friend, to Robert Owen four days before the Kennington meeting is an unambiguous declaration for revolution: 'any attempt to stop short' he wrote 'will be suicidal...'[294]

Bronterre O'Brien resigned the Convention because he felt that some of his colleagues were 'going too fast.' Julian Harney, his insurrectionary hackles up, spoke to the Irish Confederates assembled on the Common of 'regeneration [of] this country,' but as all at Kennington Common were unarmed at the Convention's bidding, it was not possible to 'dispute with the armed forces in possession of the bridges.'[295] And although Ernest Jones went along with O'Connor's appeal for the crowd to peacefully disperse, there is evidence sufficient to say he fumed for weeks afterwards at the climb down.

The National Convention was making all the right constitutional noises, yet the idea that something cataclysmic must occur to bring an outcome of one sort or another was surely present in the minds of a good many Chartists and Confederates on that Monday morning. William Cuffay saw it that way. He was not alone in seeing the need to draw out the army from behind the civilian lines of police and special constables in order to reveal government oppression to a watching world; he urged the crowd to march upon Westminster after O'Connor had spoken against it. Everyone, ruling and ruled, understood the implications of a conflict of soldier against civilian in the capital: a clear sign of revolution. There was no drawn plan for it, but revolutions do not entirely rely upon plans. John Mitchel understood this and spoke of it. As it turns out, the event which could well have sparked it, a determined march on the House of Commons at Westminster, was avoided. Monday 10th April 1848 was indeed an extraordinarily significant day in the history of Britain. Comparing its potential with its outcome, it is no wonder the authorities were elated by their success that day. It was a poker game played for a nation, the government's winning card being O'Connor's influence over the crowd.

And so, having not drawn out the soldiers on April 10th, it was the last days of May and the first days of June, directly following the conviction of John Mitchel and opening with the great march through the night time streets of London, which next were the days of great threat to the established order. These were days of real opportunity to the insurgents because their actions had a certain spontaneity to them. If a rising were ever to occur this probably was the time, when tens of thousands were on the streets and the will was high. But there was an obvious lack not only of decisive leadership but of visible leadership during this time when the people were out. Leading London Confederate Thomas Daly was on Clerkenwell Green for the second night's demonstrations but it seems he did not appear again, and when he quit London for Paris, he left the field to Francis Looney, Charles McCarthy, and subordinates like William Dowling and Robert Crowe. In these tumultuous days of the first week of June everyone was waiting for news of a rising in Ireland yet, crucially, Chartist planning was focused, hopes pinned on a week hence, 12th June, when Peter McDouall was to take charge of the Bonner's Field meeting by which time that 'subtle electric force whose influence evades arithmetic' – spoken of by Charles Gavan Duffy at the time of Ireland's attempt – had passed unavailed in the streets of London.

What is more, those who gathered on the streets from 29th May to 4th June were willing to try but were not sufficiently ready. This unpreparedness was often heard being voiced by those who assembled. The great sprawl of London made it nigh impossible for these people to coalesce and they needed leadership when the Chartist leaders were faced with the imminent danger of their own arrests. Alexander Sharp's talk of absentee speakers at the Bonners' Field meeting of 4th June, and the formation at this time of the secretive Ulterior Committee give every indication that the Chartist leaders feared for their own safety and were divided amongst themselves over which direction to take, while a potential uprising, offering itself in the streets of London, came and went unavailed.

Peter McDouall had clearly accepted by this time that there was only one course before him: insurrection. He attended the Ulterior Committee's second meeting immediately after the abandonment of the 12th June meeting on Bonner's Field; a prearrangement which gives a clear indication of the direction of his thoughts in the dangerous days running-up to the 12th. But exactly what occurred a few days later to make him abandon his plan to raise barricades in London and to cause conflagration remains a mystery.

As to the August plot, there is an even deeper sense of anger and despair attached to this as by now the contest had been won by the authorities, in France and in Britain. Those remaining at liberty and who were involved in the plot would surely have known in their hearts that the execution of the thing was beyond possibility; that, to quote William Cuffay, 'the halter was round their necks.' They surely dreamed of liberty, equality, fraternity while knowing that a last desperate strike against the authorities was what they were really embarked upon.

Whatever was in their minds, the area of London which these revolutionaries would have had to take, six miles of it from the city to Westminster, is a field of action so large that something miraculous would have been needed to successfully coordinate and carry through a rising of undisciplined men, women and youths. And this miracle would have had to be replicated in Birmingham, Manchester, Liverpool, as well as the centres of Scotland and Wales. Even so, plans were laid. It was all that was left this rump of Chartist organisation to try.

Had they from the start had the middle classes with them it might have been a different matter, but there is something in the isolation of the Chartists from the middle classes which put the possibility of successful revolutionary action in Britain beyond reach. In 1848 the middle classes were firmly with the British authorities. Had the planned insurrection broken out, a civil war with one class fighting the others in a perfectly unequal contest would have ensued.

And throughout it all, the part played by London's Metropolitan police force and those of the provinces cannot be overstated. These organisations played a decisive role in the failure of revolutionary ambitions. They were the buffer between the people and the military and their utility to the government as a source of social control was invaluable to the propertied classes. The revolutionaries of 1848 could hear the music but lacked the instruments and the hall in which to play it.

Closer to ground, Julian Harney felt that the people expected to do the rising were too politically ignorant to sustain the level of activity seen in Italy, France, Germany, Hungary, Austria, Poland.[296] Edward Royle describes earlier revolutionary movements in England as tending to arise from economic hardship rather than from political conviction, Dorothy Thompson, writing in 2005, identified the grievances of the Chartist period as social rather than political, and David Goodway says of London Chartism that it was 'intrinsically backward-looking' and 'not a confident, proletarian anticipation of socialism'.[297] Perhaps a sense of the legendary legitimacy thought to be possessed by the British authorities, at least in comparison with continental authorities, cast its magic over the poor and disaffected as it did over the wealthy and well-placed. Appeals from the powerless and dispossessed might not be listened to in Britain, but at least the right to appeal was there. Guiseppe Mazzini recognised this. He is remembered to have said at a London meeting of the People's International League in 1847 that the necessity to revolt was not as strong in Britain as in Italy (he would not have included Ireland in this).[298] 'You have had your grand decisive struggle against Tyrannous Power. Your fathers brought it to the block; and you have now a Representation, and you have Charters and Written Rights to appeal to...But what are my countrymen to do, who are trodden down under the iron heel of a foreign tyranny?'[299]

At the end there were, of course, the James Bezers and William Cuffays, the George Mullins, William Laceys and Joseph Richies who were ready to make a final effort on behalf of their class; also the many unknowns represented by men like the sabred Dunkard, and the many more unknowns whom Julian Harney perceived as not possessing political know-how but who understood the penalties of poverty. Furthermore, Julian Harney thought it was indecisive and fractured leadership which propelled them all into hopeless action for which they paid dear.

George Julian Harney had a long time in which to dwell upon these matters for he lived nearly fifty years beyond the revolutions of 1848, long enough to see the foundation of England's Independent Labour Party in 1893. He did not, though, stay in London beyond the mid-1850s. London lost its purpose to him. Ernest Jones fell out with him, Bronterre O'Brien fell out with him, and his friendships with Friedrich Engels and Karl Marx took a wrong turn. For Marx and Engels, Harney was not sufficiently partisan. In the same spirit in which he had printed Engels' pieces in the early 1840s so he continued to insert the views of those whom Marx and Engels disliked, so that they too fell out with him. He said of himself that he was not a leader, that he knew nothing of arms, had 'no stomach for fighting, and would rather die after some other fashion than by bullet or rope.'[300] Julian Harney was a man who brought others together but never with the intention of holding them together: that was not part of his gift. He was a communicator. In fact, he was *the* communicator between the British radical movement and the continental democratic and socialist movements during the late 1830s, 1840s and early 1850s. It was he who first published Helen Macfarlane's English translation of the *Communist Manifesto* in his London-based paper *The Red Republican* in 1850.

On 11th February 1853 Mary Cameron Harney died at Mauchline Ayrshire. Harney's friend George Jacob Holyoake had once described her as 'tall, beautiful, and of high spirit.'[301] 'At this hour,' wrote Harney, with 'a future, gloomy, uncertain, impenetrable weighing upon me, sorely and sadly I feel the want of her admirable counsel.'[302] With his work failing, with his wife gone, he left London where so much had happened to engage his years of youth.

He began working with Joseph Cowen at Newcastle-upon-Tyne. Cowen was a rising middle class industrialist, liberal and republican. This collaboration went on for two years. Three years after that, in 1858, Harney attended the founding event in London of Ernest Jones' Manhood Suffrage movement which embraced class co-operation – something he would not have dreamed of twenty years earlier when he was a self-declared insurrectionist. By now he was living on the Isle of Jersey and seems to have been happy there; he grew a long beard and continued his writing and editing. He remarried and left Jersey for America in May 1863 to spend some thirteen years working in Boston as a clerk in the civil service, and so he became a self-condemned exile of sorts and learned that America was not the hope of the world as he had thought. James Bronterre O'Brien died during Harney's time in Boston, and news of Ernest Jones' death in 1868 brought him to tears on a Boston street.[303]

He ended his days living by himself at Richmond some ten miles west of London, and although the fight for social and political change in which he had engaged as a very young man did not produce the results he wanted to see – societies fashioned by the dictates of those who laboured to create the wealth – his disappointment did not prevent him from choosing to live in a room festooned with memories of that lost fight. On the wall by his bed were portraits of Feargus O'Connor, Joseph Cowen, Richard Oastler, William Lovett who had drawn up the People's Charter in 1837, Friedrich Engels, Karl Marx and others. The space above the mantelpiece was taken up with portraits of literary men: Byron, Scott, Burns, Shelley, Moore and, placed above them all, William Shakespeare. There was a framed letter from William Cobbett and beside that an image of Cobbett's daughter Eleanor, then, on the wall of the sunny south-facing window were more faces: Darwin, Ruskin, Sidney, Chaucer, Raleigh, De Stael, Mary Wollstonecraft.[304]

George Julian Harney died on the Thursday morning of 9th December 1897 aged eighty and he was probably quite glad to go. A few weeks before his death he had been asked by a visitor to recount his Chartist days but as none of them had ever fallen into place for him, he simply concluded that: 'One may live too long.'[305] He started out as a revolutionary idealist, and ended his days as something of a conservative realist.

Harney would not have been surprised at some of the obituaries he received. Many inclined to slight denigration of him because of what they called his changed politics. He might, though, have been mildly satisfied with the letter which appeared in London's *Morning Post* on 14th December 1897:

'As to the remark of a contemporary that Harney and Cowen and other Chartists became Conservatives in their latter days...should it not be rather said that latter-day Conservatism is a good deal Chartist? Let us be fair and remember that property qualification of members has been abolished, that vote by ballot has been established, that Tory household suffrage is an approximate to Chartist Manhood Suffrage, and that [the benefit of] equal electoral districts has been approximated by the last Redistribution of Seats...'[306]

The constitutional changes for which so many Chartists plotted revolution in 1848 and for which they were transported, imprisoned or died, had as good as been gained by the end of the century. As to Ireland, the fight for Repeal of the Union resulted in the island's partition in 1921 which was not what the Confederates of 1848 rebelled for, nor did they want to see the religious partisanship which beleaguers humanity still and which, in one guise or another, looks set to continue to do so into the distant future.

20
The After Story

There is one well-worn epithet applying to this thing called history which states that it is written by the victors. The British government and those they represented were the victors in the 1848 battle which they waged against the democratic-socialist Chartists, and their version of what happened in 1848 prevailed for more than one hundred years. The victors' version of the Irish Confederates' story lingers on to this day.

The Confederate experience of 1848 was different from the Chartist. Rebellion was the only course left open to the Irish. The attempted rebellion in Ireland in 1848 in the depths of the famine was undertaken by the Confederate leaders when they perfectly knew that their action was hopeless. They were propelled into their attempt by the British parliament's suspension of the Act of Habeas Corpus for Ireland. The rebellion has ever since been portrayed as a ridiculous affair and is still sometimes referred to as 'The Battle of Widow McCormac's Cabbage Patch'. This derisory title arose from early newspaper reports that Margaret McCormac, when her house was taken over by the police on the decisive day of the rebellion at Boulagh Commons, had gone to Smith O'Brien to appeal to him to diffuse the situation by talking to the police barricaded within and so save her children who were kept there. It is said she found him crouched in her cabbage garden to avoid fire from the police.[307] And so the tragic events which unfolded that day with men killed, children held terrified and bereft while their home was ripped apart inside and out, and the future of an entire nation foretold by the desperate act of desperate men produced by desperate national circumstances, all were soon being referred to as nothing more than the battle of a cabbage patch.

As to Chartism, the victors dwelt entirely on their success over the Chartists on Monday 10th April 1848 when the great crowd assembled on Kennington Common was prevented, through show of overwhelming force, from marching on Westminster to deliver the petition for political reform and was obliged to retreat, collective tail between collective leg. '[T]heir insignificance was demonstrated, and their menaces rendered impotent by the firm and imposing attitude of the loyal and well-affected inhabitants arranged in defence of peace, property, and order.' So, the *Annual Register* of 1848 summed up that year's Chartist activities.[308] The extensive disturbances and subsequent plans of the late spring and summer to set London ablaze by men with nothing left to lose were allowed to be forgotten as 'pothouse' conspiracies.

The Whig government and civil authorities of 1848 portrayed the Chartist leaders as insidious, designing individuals who misled their working-class followers in order to advance their own political ends. As a notion it worked to put aside all justifiable argument for political reform in 1848. Court prosecutors and judges played on this during the summer and autumn trials of that year. Very likely, these men actually believed what they said; the bulk of the propertied classes probably thought of the Chartists in one-dimensional terms, as a wretched and uneducated mass led by Machiavellian political agitators bent on revolution for their own aggrandisement. This together with newspaper editorials and fictional representations of Chartism had much to do with the obscuring for generations of the events of 1848.

The non-radical presses of 1848 promoted the same notions while describing disaffected Londoners as a 'rabble' and a 'mob'. London's *Morning Chronicle* dubbed men like Peter McDouall and Ernest Jones 'selfish, reckless and dangerous.'[309] The 1850 novel *Alton Locke, Tailor and Poet* written by Charles Kingsley (open-minded church man sympathetic to Chartist aims and future author of *Water Babies*) portrayed the rank and file Chartists of 1848 as dupes. Kingsley used the experience of Chartist Thomas Cooper as the basis for his protagonist Alton Locke, a misguided young man who spends his prison time learning the folly of his Chartist ways upon which he returns to the church as his guide – Kingsley's personal solution to this great social issue.[310] And so, an Irish cabbage patch battle and misguided British mechanics led by unprincipled adventurers were the stories which prevailed of the people who gave their all in the fight for independence, democracy and a better life. It was not until the latter half of the twentieth century that Dorothy Thompson's pre-eminent work on Chartism restored to the story its proper balance. Chartism's good cause, dignity and significance re-emerged from what can properly be described as the victors' calumny.[311]

Yet in 1848 there were men like the bricklayer Joseph Richie, a Chartist class-leader, who was prepared to manufacture in the back-street kitchen where he lived weapons of terror in order to awaken to a warring society the appalling lives led by thousands upon thousands of working people: the fire bombs found at the Orange Tree on 17th August 1848 are reported to each have contained two and a half ounces of gunpowder and old nails.[312] Perhaps it is possible, one hundred and seventy years later, to glimpse and to vaguely understand the acts of Chartists, Confederates, revolutionaries, politicians and the civil authorities of 1848, through the simple telling of the stories of those individuals who played their part in it all: those who thought themselves able to attack horse and rider with pikes on Britain's city streets but never did, those who thought themselves ready to throw fire-bombs but never did, and those who set about to defend themselves against the dreaded, pike-wielding spectre of a rising working class.

ARRESTS OF PROMINENT LONDON CHARTISTS AND CONFEDERATES

June arrests:

John Fussell, Chartist, aged 32, jeweller's assistant, living Corporation Row, Clerkenwell. Arrested 7 June 1848, charged with attending an unlawful meeting. Trial opened 5th July 1848 on eight counts including sedition, being present at an unlawful assembly and for riot. Sentenced to two years' imprisonment for sedition, three months' imprisonment for unlawful assembly.

Joseph Williams, Chartist, aged 40, baker. Arrested 7 June 1848, charged with using seditious language. Trial opened 6 July 1848 on charges of forming part of an unlawful assembly and with riot. Sentenced to two years and one week's imprisonment.

Ernest Jones, Chartist, aged 28, lawyer and writer. Arrested 7 June 1848 at Manchester, charged with sedition. Tried 10 July 1848 at Central Criminal Court. Sentenced to two years' imprisonment.

William John Vernon, Chartist, lecturer on mesmerism and phrenology, aged 40. Arrested 8 June 1848 for attending an unlawful meeting. Trial opened 6 July 1848 charged with forming part of an unlawful assembly and with riot. Sentenced to two years' imprisonment.

Alexander Sharp, Chartist, aged 27, copper-plate printer, living St Georges Road, St Luke's (?). Arrested 7 June 1848. Trial opened 7th July charged with using seditious language. Sentenced to two years' imprisonment for sedition and three months' imprisonment for unlawful assembly.

Francis Looney, Confederate, cabinet maker, age 34. Arrested early in June 1848 and charged with seditious speech. Trial opened 8th July 1848. Sentenced to two years' imprisonment for sedition, and two months' imprisonment for unlawful assembly.

July arrest:

Peter Murray McDouall, Chartist, age 35 (?), medical doctor. Arrested 21 July 1848 in the early hours at Ashton-under-Lyne.

Trial commenced 28 August 1848 at Lancashire Assizes, Liverpool, charged with sedition and conspiracy. Sentenced to two years imprisonment.

August arrests:

Robert Crowe, Confederate, tailor, age 25, living 1 Archer Street, Camden Town. Arrested first week of August 1848. Charged with seditious language. Trial opened 26 August 1848. Sentenced to two years' imprisonment.

Henry Argue, Confederate, 23 shoemaker. Arrested 17 August 1848. Trial opened 22 Sept 1848. Sentenced to two years' imprisonment.

William Cuffay, Chartist, tailor, age 60, living Soho. Arrested 18 August. Trial opened 25 September. Sentenced to life transportation.

Thomas Fay, Chartist, age 20, closer. Arrested 18 August. Trial opened 25 September. Sentenced to life transportation.

William Lacey, Chartist, age 38, bootmaker. Arrested mid-August. Trial opened 25 September. Sentenced to life transportation.

William Dowling, Confederate, artist, living 5 Nassau Street. Arrested 20 August 1848. Trial opened 25 September 1848 on charge of sedition. Sentenced to life transportation.

George Shell, Chartist, aged 32, bootmaker. Trial opened late August 1848 on a charge of sedition. Sentenced to two years' imprisonment.

James Maxwell Bryson, Chartist, dentist. Trial opened late August 1848 on a charge of sedition. Sentenced to two years' imprisonment.

[John] James Bezer, Chartist, aged 32, street fish seller. Arrested mid-August. Trial opened 28 August on a charge of sedition. Sentenced to two years' imprisonment.

John Shaw, Chartist, aged 41, undertaker. Arrested 22 August. Trial opened 20 September for sedition. Sentenced to two years' imprisonment.

Orange Tree arrests, 17 August 1848, trial opened 22 September 1848.

Joseph Richie, Chartist, aged 42, bricklayer, living No 2, Cross Court, Russell Court, Drury Lane. Arrested 17 August. Trial opened 22 September 1848. Sentenced to life transportation.

Alfred Able, aged 23, porter. Sentenced to two years' imprisonment.

William Gurney, aged 42, shoemaker. Sentenced to two years' imprisonment.

John Sheppard, aged 34, tailor. To enter into recognizances to appear if called upon.

James Snowball, aged 32, joiner. Sentenced to two years' imprisonment.

James Richardson, aged 30, joiner.

George Greenslade, aged 30, shoemaker. To enter into recognizances to appear if called upon.

Henry Small, aged 31, joiner. To enter into recognizances to appear if called upon.

Edward Scadding, aged 28, brass turner, living 31 Cock Lane, Smithfield. Sentenced to two years' imprisonment.

William Byrne, aged 44, shoemaker. To enter into recognizances to appear if called upon.

Philip Martin, aged 45, newsman. Sentenced to two years' imprisonment.

Angel Public House arrests, 17 August 1848, trial opened 29 September 1848.

Charles Taylor, labourer, aged 22. To enter into recognizances to appear when called upon.

George Cox, shoemaker, aged 23. To enter into recognizances to appear if called upon.

William Poole, shoemaker, aged 38. Living No. 8, Northampton Place, Walworth. Sentenced to eighteen months' imprisonment.

Charles Wicks, no ready information.

Thomas Herbert, tanner, aged 21. Sentenced to eighteen months' imprisonment.

Thomas Ions (Irons), labourer, aged 33. Sentenced to eighteen months' imprisonment.

James Browton (Prowton), labourer, aged 29. Sentenced to two years' imprisonment.

Hugh Conway, typefounder, aged 27. Sentenced to two years' imprisonment.

Alexander Hardy, shoemaker, aged 29. To enter into recognizances to appear if called upon.

Samuel Hardy, shoemaker, aged 29. To enter into recognizances to appear if called upon.

James John Norton, smith, aged 30. To enter into recognizances to appear if called upon.

William Winspere, labourer, aged 26. Sentenced to two years' imprisonment.

Samuel Morgan, cigar maker, aged 22. Sentenced to imprisonment.

Blue Anchor arrests, 17 August 1848

Thomas Jones, shoemaker, aged 32

Frederick Stone

William Swinbourne

Charles Young, shoemaker, aged 38. Sentenced to eighteen months' imprisonment

Thomas Elliot (a youth)

September arrest:

George Bridge Mullins, age 22, surgeon's apprentice, living 34 Southampton Street, Strand. Arrested 18 September 1848. Trial opened 28 October 1848. Sentenced to transportation.

REFERENCES AND ANNOTATIONS

1   *The Northern Star* 5 Feb 1848 'The Democratic Movement in France' (probably written by Friedrich Engles); *The Times* 4 Feb 1848, 'Express from Paris'. Sicily had already successfully risen against control from Naples. This hardened the resolve of the Italian north.
2   Vincent, David (ed), (1977) pp. 149-87
3   Saville, John (1987) p. 34
4   For the Irish situation *see* Townshend, Charles, (1984) *Political Violence in Ireland,* Oxford University Press
5   Gammage, R.G. (1984) p. 67
6   Black, David, Playpus Review (Dec 2011) pp. 2, 4
7   Charles Greville in Pearce, Edward (ed) (2006) p. 262
8   Duffy, Charles Gavan (1883) p. 535
9   *Hansard,* 24 Feb, 1848 vol 96, cc1245-1246
10   Ó Corráin, D. & T. O'Riordan (2011) p. 61
11   Dillon, William (1888) p. 96
12   Dillon, William (1888) pp. 146-7
13   letter from Captain Wynne, British officer, in Percival, John, (1995) p.70
14   letter from Charles Edward Trevelyan to Sir Randolf Routh Commissary General in Ireland, 21 July 1846, in Woodham Smith (1962) p. 89
15   *Hansard,* 1 Feb 1847, vol 89, cc636-637
16   for New York details: Laxton, Edward (1997) p. 26; for Liverpool details: Ó Corráin, D. & T. O'Riordan (2011) p. 79
17   Gladstone, writing on 12 Oct 1845, in Shannon, Richard (1982) p. 183
18   Ó Corráin, D. & T. O'Riordan (2011) p. 59
19   Read, Stuart J. (1895) p. 91
20   Carl Welcker quoted in Blackbourn (1997) p. 98
21   *The Diary of Ernest Jones 1839-47* in 'Our History' Pamphlet 21 (1961) p. 12, Self Mark A61,held at the Working Class Movement Library, Salford

22   *The Diary of Ernest Jones 1839-47* in 'Our History' Pamphlet 21 (1961) p. 17 Self Mark A61,held at the Working Class Movement Library, Salford

23   From *The Song of the Factory Slave*, in Cole, G.D.H, (1941) p. 337

24   Feargus O'Connor's letters of Jan 4 1848 and Jan 6 1848, in Black F.G. & R.M. Black (eds) (!969) , p. 61-2

25   *Northern Star and National Trades' Journal* 1 April 1848 'The Fraternal Democrates'

26   Schoyen, A.R. (1958) p. 136

27   *Newcastle Weekly Chronicle* 17 August 1895, quoted in Schoyen, A.R. (1958) p. 129; Aveling (1897) p. 8

28   Engels, Friedrich, (2009 edition) pp. 57, 60-62

29   Engels, Friedrich, (2009 edition) p. 40

30   Engels, Friedrich, (2009 edition) pp. 40-5

31   19 Feb 1848, microfiche X023/107 held at London Metropolitan Archives

32   Feargus O'Connor's letter, May 1846, The Allsop Collection: Coll Misc 525, files 1-4, letter 9, held at the British Library of Political and Economic Science, London

33   *Northern Star and National Trades' Journal*, 22 January 1848, 'Metropolitan Chartist Hall'

34   *Northern Star and National Trades' Journal* 1 July 1848, 'Address of the Executive to the People'

35   in Read, D and E Glasgow, (1961) p. 124

36   Duffy, Charles Gavan, (1883) p. 543 & p. 547

37   Koseki, Takashir, pp. 16-17

38   *Manchester Times and Gazette* 25 March 1848 'Chartist and Repeal Demonstrations'

39   *Northern Star and National Trades' Journal*, 25 March 1848, 'Great Meeting at Manchester'

40   *Freeman's Journal* 22 March 1838 'Prosecutions'

41   *Hansard* 8 February 1847, vol 89 c943

42   *Hansard* 9 Feb 1848, vol 96, c312

43   *Hansard* 9 Feb 1848, vol 96, c352

44   *Hansard* 9 March 1848, vol 97 c346

45   *Hansard* 24 March 1848, vol 97, c1012

46 *see* Goodway, David (1982) p. 66

47 *Morning Chronicle* 7 March 1848 'The Income Tax – Open Air Meeting in Trafalgar-Square'

48 *Morning Post,* 7 March 1848, 'The Income-Tax – Open Air Meeting in Trafalgar-Square'

49 Malmesbury, James Howard Harris, (1884) p. 161

50 Pearce, Edward (2006) p. 261-2

51 HO45/2410 Part 1, doc 280

52 Saville, John (1987) p. 103

53 *Northern Star and National Trades' Journal* 8 April 1848 'The National Convention'

54 in Plummer, Alfred, (1971) pp.182 & 191

55 *Northern Star and National Trades' Journal* 8 April 1848 'The National Convention'

56 Malmesbury, James Howard Harris, (1884) p. 165

57 Goodway, David (1982) pp. 73, 130-36

58 *Northern Star and National Trades' Journal* 8 April 1848, p. 8: 'The National Convention'

59 *Northern Star and National Trades' Journal* 15 April 1848 'National Convention'

60 an example of this is in Howe, Catherine (2014) pp. 114-15

61 *Northern Star and National Trades' Journal* 8 April 1848, p.8: 'The National Convention'

62 *Northern Star and National Trades' Journal* 8 April 1848, p. 5 'The National Convention'

63 *The Times* 8 April 1848

64 George Julian Harney's letter of 28 March 1849, in Black F.G. & R.M.(eds) (1969) p. 250

65 Benson, C. and Viscount Esher, (1908) p.167

66 Woodham-Smith gives a comprehensive and balanced account of the situation in Ireland running up to 1848, (pp 310-29)

67 *Northern Star and National Trades' Journal* 25 March 1848 'The State of Ireland'

68 *The Times,* 8 April 1848 'The gentlemen who have kindly undertaken to'

69 Cooper, Thomas, (1872) (1971 edition) p.304

70   *Northern Star and National Trades' Journal* 8 April 1848

71   *Northern Star and National Trades' Journal* 8 April 1848 p. 1

72   *Morning Chronicle* 10 April 1848, 'Meeting in Victoria Park'

73   Mackay, Charles, (1877) p. 57

74   HO45/2410 Part 1 doc 453

75   *Northern Star and National Trades' Journal* 15 April 1848, p. 1

76   Feargus O'Connor's letter 5 May 1848 to Thomas Allsop, Allsop Collection Misc. 525 files 1-4; Roberts, Stephen (1999) pp. 111-14; *The Times* 11 April 1848 'Kennington-Common'

77   *The Times* 11 April 1848

78   For Ernest Jones' comment: *Northern Star and National Trades' Journal* 10 June 1848 'Arrest of Chartist Leaders'

79   HO45/2410 Part 1 docs 507 & 460

80   HO45/2410 Part 1 doc 544

81   Goodway, David, (1982) p. 76

82   HO45/2410 Part 1 doc 453

83   Gammage, R.G. (1894) (2012 facsimile) p. 315

84   *Northern Star and National Trades' Journal* 15 April 1848 pp. 6-7

85   HO45/2410 Part 1

86   in Harte, Liam (2011) p. 39

87   *Northern Star and National Trades' Journal* 15 April 1848, p. 5 'Brutality of the Police'

88   HO45/2410 doc 460

89   *Northern Star and National Trades' Journal* 15 April 1848 'National Convention'

90   Thomas Allsop's letter of 6 April 1848 to Robert Owen, held in the Robert Owen Collection at Holyoake House, Manchester

91   Plummer, Alfred (1971) p. 192

92   *Morning Chronicle*, 11 April 1848, p. 4 col 5

93   in Goodway, (1982) p. 79

94   in Woodham-Smith (1962) p. 321

95   in Woodham-Smith (1962) p.340

96 *Hansard* 10 April 1848 vol 98 cc73-75; *Morning Post* 11 April 1848, 'Imperial Parliament'

97 *Hansard* 10 April 1848 vol 98 cc85-86. The Treason Felony Act of 1848 still stands as active legislation although part of it is said to be incompatible with Article 10 of the European Convention on Human Rights. In 2000 Alan Rusbridger and Polly Toynbee of *The Guardian* newspaper asked the Attorney General to clarify the interpretation of section 3 of the 1848 Act in light of the Human Rights Act of 1998, this prior to their publication of articles advocating the abolition of the monarchy which is in contravention of the 1848 Act. Mr Rusbridger asked the Attorney General whether or not a prosecution would be brought if they were to publish. No prosecution resulted when, on 6th December 2000, the articles appeared in *The Guardian*. (26 June 2003, House of Lords)

98 *Hansard* 13 April 1848 vol 98 cc284-288

99 *Hansard* 13 April 1848 vol 98 cc291-29

100 Harney's letter of 30 March 1849 to Engels, in Black F.G. & R.M. Black p. 240

101 This is a different John Shaw from the delegate for Leeds at the April Convention.

102 *Northern Star and National Trades' Journal* Sept 30 1848 'The Chartist Trials'

103 *Northern Star and National Trades' Journal* 6 May 1848 pp. 6-7

104 McDouall, Peter, 24 April 1841

105 *Northern Star and National Trades' Journal* 13 May 1848 'National Assembly'

106 *Freemans Journal* 27 April 1848 'Mr W.S.O'Brien'

107 *Hansard* 29 May 1848 vol 99 cc2-3

108 *Northern Star and National Trades' Journal* 27 May 1848 'The Provisional Executive Committee to the people'

109 for more on the Metropolitan Police Force in 1848 *see* Goodway (1982) pp. 99-105

110 *Northern Star and National Trades' Journal* 10 April 1848 'The Police'

111 *Bradford Observer,* 23 May 1839, p. 4, col 2

112 For more on the actions at Bradford *see* Wright, D.G. *The Chartist Risings in Bradford*

113 *Northern Star and National Trades' Journal* 10 June 1848, 'Arrest of Chartist Leaders'; *Northern Star and National Trades' Journal* 17 June 1848, 'Letter from Mr John Fussell to his Brother'. In *London Chartism 1848* David Goodway quotes John Russell's letter to Queen Victoria, written at this time, explaining that 'In order to prosecute for seditious words, a reporter of the govt must be present . . .' Goodway goes on to say that because the government did not have this evidence against Fussell 'the difficulty was overcome by resorting to the evidence from the [freelance] newspaper reporters present at the time of Fussell's speech. (Goodway, D. 1982, pp. 84-5) *See also* Central Criminal Court t18480703-1677.

114 *Northern Star and National Trades' Journal* 10 June for J. Williams, 'Arrest of Chartist Leaders'

115 Goodway (1982) pp.81-2. The number was 12,000 in *The Morning Chronicle* of 30 May 1848; 150,000 according to Alexander Sharp (Central Criminal Court Ref: t18480703-1712)

116 *Northern Star and National Trades' Journal* 3 June 1848 'Chartism and Repeal in the Metropolis'

117 Central Criminal Court: Old Bailey Ref: t18480703-1677; Williams' and Vernon's speeches *The Times* 7 July 1848 'Central Criminal Court July 6th'

118 HO45/2410 Part 1 docs 468, 471. For George Davis's activities: *The Times*, 30 October 1848 'The Chartist Trials'

119 *Northern Star and National Trades' Journal* 3 June 1848 'The Supremacy of the Law Demonstrated'

120 *Northern Star and National Trades' Journal* 3 June 1848 'Chartism and Repeal in the Metropolis'

121 *Morning Post,* 1 June 1848 'The Chartist Demonstration'

122 *Morning Chronicle* 1 June 1848 'Chartist Proceedings

123 HO 45/2410 Part 1 doc 472

124 *Morning Post* 2 June 1848 'The Chartist Disturbances'

125 *Morning Post* 3 June 1848, 'The Chartist Disturbances'

126 HO45/2410 Part 1 doc 484-5

127 *Morning Chronicle* 5 June 1848 'The Charists – Renewed Disturbances'; HO45/2104 Part 1 doc 478

128 *Morning Chronicle* 5 June 1848 'The Chartists – Renewed Disturbances'

129 *Northern Star and National Trades' Journal* June 10 1848 'Arrest of Chartist leaders'; Hansard 8 June 1848 vol 99 cc506; Central Criminal Court t18480703-1730

130 TS/11 doc 23

131 Central Criminal Court t18480703-1712 for the James Waller details; TS/11 doc 24 for the Curtis details

132 *Morning Chronicle* 5 June 1848 'The Chartists, Renewed Disturbances'

133 TS11 doc 26; Central Criminal Court Ref: t18480703-1712

134 *Morning Chronicle*, 5 June 1848 'The Chartists – Renewed Disturbances'

135 *Morning Chronicle* 5 June 1848, 'Capture of a Chartist Leader'

136 *Standard* 5 June 1848 'Multiple News Item' col 3

137 Hansard 5 June 1848 vol 99 cc337-8

138 Hansard 8 June 1848 vol 99 cc507-508

139 *Northern Star and National Trades' Journal* 10 June 'The London Repealers'

140 Goodway, David (1982), p.228

141 *Northern Star and National Trades' Journal* June 10 1848 'Arrest of Chartist Leaders'

142 HO45/2410 Part 1

143 HO45/2410 Part 1 doc 496

144 *Standard* 10 July 1848 'The Chartist Trials'

145 HO45/2410 Part 1 docs 604 & 671 for inventories; HO45/2410 Part 1 doc 744 for letter

146 MEPO 2/59; *Morning Post* 12 June 1848 'The Chartists'

147 Goodway, David, (1982), p. 144-5

148 Goodway, David, (1982), p. 86

149 *Northern Star and National Trades' Journal* 17 June 1848 'Government demonstration against Chartists'

150 *Ibid*

151 Goodway, David, (1982), pp. 87-8, 228, 267 n431

152 HO45/2410 Part 1 doc 503

153 Goodway, David, (1982), pp. 88-9

154 HO45/2410 Part 2, doc 793

155 *Hansard* 4 August vol 100 cc1153-4; Greville, Charles in Pearce, Edward (2006) p. 266 (entry of 10th June 1848) for the military citation.

156 Charles Gavan Duffy lists the Confederate Council members as T.F. Meagher, Father Kenyon, William Smith O'Brien, C.G.Duffy, John Dillon, Richard O'Gorman, Frank Morgan, P.J.Smyth, John Martin, Michael Doheny, Dr Kane of Kilkenny, James Cantwell, Denny Lane of Cork, M.J.Barry, R.D.Williams, John Byrne, B.Dowling of Limerick, Michael Crean and John Rainor (Duffy, (1883) p. 611n)

157 *Hansard* 22 July 1848 vol 100 cc702-703

158 Meagher's memoir of 1848, in Cavanagh, Michael (1892), p.251

159 Woodham-Smith (1962) pp. 362, 363

160 Duffy, Charles Gavan (1883) pp. 549-50, 598, 695

161 Meagher in Doheny Ch VII (unpaged)

162 Duffy, Charles Gavan (1883) p. 652-3; Meagher in Cavanghan p. 264

163 Duffy, Charles Gavan (1883) p. 648.

164 *Memoir of Charles Kickham*, in Duffy, Charles Gavan (1883) p. 682-3

165 Duffy, Charles Gavan (1883) p. 663 & 667

166 *Hansard* 27 July 1848 vol 100 cc914-5. It was known by the Chartist leadership that the government were suppressing press reports of unrest in Ireland. See reports on Ernest Jones, Central Criminal Court t18480703-1730

167 *Morning Chronicle* 26 July 1848 'Meeting of Irish Repealers'

168 *The Times* 27 July 1848 'Chartist Meeting in Cripplegate'; *Morning Chronicle* 27 July 1848 'Chartist Meeting at the Theatre, Milton-Street'

169 *Lloyd's Weekly London Newspaper* 27 August 1848 'Another Committal for Sedition'

170 *The Times* 8 June 1848 'It really gives the greatest concern'

171 Duffy, Charles Gavan (1883) p. 687; *Jackson's Oxford Journal* 5 Aug 1848 'The Rebellion in Ireland'.

172 *Belfast News-Letter* 22 August 1848 'The Revolutionary Movement'. The War House Museum is housed in the McCormac farmhouse, The Commons. John Kavangh was killed during the American Civil War at the Sunken Road, Antietam on 17th September 1862.

173 *Morning Chronicle* 3 Aug 1848 'Ireland'

174 in Duffy, Charles Gavan (1883) p. 669n

175 *The Examiner* 29 July 1848 'Later news from Ireland'

176 *Times* 28 Aug 1848. 'Old Court'; *Northern Star and National Trades' Journal* 12 August 1848 'Arrest of another London Chartist'

177 *Northern Star and National Trades' Journal* July 15 1848 'The Executive Council to the People'

178 *Ibid*

179 in Quennel, Peter, (1988) p. 164

180 in Quennel, Peter, (1988) p. 370

181 in Vincent, David (ed) (1977) p. 163

182 Goodway, David, (1982), p. 91

183 Goodway, David, (1982), p. 93; *Morning Chronicle* 19 Aug 1848, 'Manchester, Friday'

184 HO45/2410 Part 1 doc 604

185 *Morning Post* 28 September 1848 'The Chartist Trials'

186 *Northern Star and National Trades' Journal* S 19 Aug 1848, 'Arrest of Armed Chartist in London'

187 *Morning Chronicle* 19 Aug 1848 'Attempted Chartist Outbreak'

188 *Northern Star and National Trades' Journal* 19 Aug 1848 'Arrest of Armed Chartists in London'

189 *Ibid*. For Young and Jones: *Morning Post*, 1 September 1848, 'Committal of Chartists'

190 Goodway, David, (1982), p. 94

191 *The Times* 18 August 1848 p. 4

192 *Morning Chronicle* 19 August 1848 'Attempted Chartist Outbreak'

193 *Ibid*

194 *Ibid*

195 *The Examiner* 30 September 1848 'Law'; During Cuffay, Fay and Lacey's trial, Powell was accused of having attempted the murder of his father in February 1840: *Morning Chronicle* 29 September 1848 'Trial of the Chartist Prisoners'

196 *Northern Star and National Trades' Journal* 19 Aug 1848 'Defence Fund'. The monies received into Peter McDouall's Defence Fund was £2.13.9.

197 *Liverpool Mercury* 29 Aug 1848 'Lancashire Assizes'

198 *Northern Star and National Trades' Journal* 2 September 1848 'Dr McDouall'

199 *Northern Star and National Trades' Journal* 10 June 1848 'The Arrests at Bingley'

200 *Northern Star and National Trades' Journal* 29 Aug 1848 'Lancashire Assizes'

201 *Morning Chronicle* 28 August 1848 'Trials for Sedition'; *Morning Post* 29 August 1848 'Central Criminal Court'

202 *Northern Star and National Trades' Journal* 27 April 1850 'South London Chartist Hall'

203 *Northern Star and National Trades' Journal* 23 September 1848 'To The Working Clases'

204 in Royle, Edward, (2000), p. 188

205 Watson, Peter, p.290

206 *Northern Star and National Trades' Journal* 17 Nov 1849 'Our Anniversary'

207 Cole, G.D.H., (1941) pp. 346-9

208 *Northern Star and National Trades' Journal* 22 July 1848 'The Press, the Law, and the People'

209 *Hansard* 25 August 1848 vol 101 cc523-7

210 *Hansard* 25 August 1848 vol 101 cc428-9

211 Mitchel, John, (1864), pp. 88-9

212 Doheny, M. (1849), (Project Gutenberg Ebook, pages unnumbered)

213 *Freeman's Journal* 20 September 1848 'Arrival of Messrs O'Brien, Meagher, Lyne, McManus, and O'Donohue'; *The Examiner* 23 Sept 'Political News'

214 *Northern Star and National Trades' Journal* 7 Oct 1848 'Conclusion of the Powell Plot'
215 *Morning Post* 20 Sept 1848 'Police Intelligence'
216 Notice of event in MEPO 2/59
217 in Royle, Edward, (2000) p. 144
218 Pearce, Edward, (ed) (2006) p. 271
219 in Vincent, David, (ed) (1977) pp. 186-7
220 *Hansard* 12 October 1831 vol 8 cc601-602
221 The Home Office letter was written on 25th January 1832 by Thomas Young, Private Secretary to George Lamb, Under-Secretary at the Home Department under Charles Grey's Whig government which sought an extention of the vote to the middle classes. The recipient was William Napier, Irishman and soldier in the British Army. In his letter Thomas Young amiably chats on about preparations to make the most of a revolution should one occur. He says how impressed he is by the energy and readiness of the people to act against the Duke of Wellington who was opposed to parliamentary reform, and he goes on: *Are you aware that, in the event of a fight, you were to be invited to take the command at Birmingham ... Parkes* [Joseph, leading political reformer and Political Unionist] *got a frank* [means of postage] *from me for you with that view, but had no occasion to send it. Had he written, I should have fired a dispatch at you with my friendly and anxious counsel and entreaty to keep you quiet and not to stir from Freshford* [Napier's home]. *It is not well to enter early into revolutions – the first fall victims. What do you think would have happened? The Reformers . . . talked big to me, and felt assured of success. The run upon the banks and the barricading of the populous country towns would have brought matters to a crisis, and a week they – the reformers – thought would have finished the business. They meant so to agitate here that no soldiers could have been spared from London . . . The most effectual blow would have been struck, and it seems difficult to have resisted the popular movement . . . The task would have been to bring society back to its former quiet state!* (Freemans Journal 7th October 1848 'The

Excluded Evidence – The Untried Traitors of '32') It is apparent that in 1831 the Home Office under Grey's Whig government was colluding with the militating Political Unions and that, in the event of an uprising, William Napier was to be offered command of the equivalent of a National Guard at Birmingham in the full knowledge of the Home Office, in the expectation that the insurrection would be put in the right direction and society brought 'back to its former quiet state' after political reform, favouring the rising middle classes, had been secured. At William Smith O'Brien's trial for treason in 1848, where William Napier appeared as a defence witness, Young's letter was not allowed as evidence by the court but was made public after sentencing.

222 in Thompson, Dorothy, (1993) p. 110
223 *Northern Star and National Trades' Journal* 16 September 1848 'What is to be done with Chartism and the Chartists?'
224 *Hansard*, 10 April 1848, vol 98 cc118
225 Joseph Hume (22 Jan 1777 – 20 Feb 1855) Scotsman and Radical politician. An advocate of free trade, trade unionism, and of religious and political reforms.
226 *Northern Star and National Trades' Journal* 13 May 1848 'Middle Class Movement'
227 *Hansard*, 20 June 1848 vol 99 cc882-883
228 *Hansard*, 20 June 1848 vol 99 cc884. (I here revert the *Hansard* report to the present tense.)
229 *Hansard*, 20 June 1848 vol 99 cc879-88
230 *Hansard*, 20 June 1848 vol 99 cc915-916; *Hansard,* 4 June 1839, vol 47 cc 136-153
231 *Daily News* 14 Aug 1849, p.5, 'Parliamentary and Financial Reform'
232 *Morning Chronicle*, 31 Oct 1848 'Central Criminal Court'
233 *Standard* 15 Nov 1848 'The Cholera'
234 *Daily News,* 11 Oct 1848 'The Cholera'
235 *Morning Chronicle* 12 January 1849 'Cholera Amongst the Pauper Children'
236 *Daily News* 5 January 1849 'Cholera at the Infant Pauper Asylum Tooting'

237 *Hansard* 12 February 1849 vol 102 cc566
238 *Northern Star and National Trades' Journal* 16 June 1849 'The Fraternal Democrats (Assembling in London) to the People of France'
239 *Northern Star and National Trades' Journal* 17 Nov 1849 'Our Anniversary'
240 *Northern Star and National Trades' Journal* 11 Nov 1848 'Chartist Organisation'
241 *Northern Star and National Trades' Journal* 2 Dec 1848 'National Victim and Defence Committee'
242 Mayhew, Henry, (1862), pp. 81-2
243 Cole, G.D.H., (1941) pp. 345-6
244 Harte, Liam, (2011) p. 40
245 *Northern Star and National Trades' Journal* 22 Sept 1849 'The Late Chartist Victims'
246 *Northern Star and National Trades' Journal* 15 Sept 1849 'Inquest on the body of Joseph Williams'
247 *Northern Star and National Trades' Journal* S 22 Sept 1849 'The Late Chartist Victims'
248 *Ibid*
249 *Northern Star and National Trades' Journal* 21 October 1848 'Whig Prisons and Chartist Prisoners'
250 Duffy, Charles Gavan, (1883) p. 464
251 Duffy, Charles Gavan, (1883) p. 612
252 Duffy, Charles Gavan, (1883) p. 471; *Freeman's Journal and Daily Commercial Advertiser* 24 September 1849 'The Cappoquin Attack'
253 in Read, Donald, (1967) p. 192
254 *Freeman's Journal* 10 July 1849 'Deportation of the State Prisoners'
255 *Northern Star and National Trades' Journal* 23 Dec 1848 'Liverpool Assizes'
256 Black, F.G. & R.M. Black (eds) (1969) p. 28
257 in Lewis, Roy and Angus Maude, (1949) p. 49
258 Jim Blake in Harte, Liam (2011) p. 62
259 for Agnes Edgell, Hollingshead, John, (1861) p. 36n

260 James Bronterre O'Brien's biographer, Alfred Plummer writes that when Hyndman 'once asked Marx how the concept of social surplus value and the social basis of exchange in social labour value occurred to him,' Marx's reply was that 'the illuminating notion . . . first arose in a co-ordinated shape from his perusal of the works of the early English Economists, Socialists and Chartists.' Bronterre O'Brien was prominent in this company. (pp.249-50, Plummer, Alfred, *Bronterre, A Political Biography of Bronterre O'Brien, 1804-1864* (1971) George Allen and Unwin). In 'The early Chartists and young Marx and Engels' (Platypus Review issue 42, December 2011 – January 2012) David Black writes 'Clearly, the Communist Manifesto could never have been written if its authors had not been engaged with English Chartists and following their fortunes very closely.' (p. 2)

261 Bronterre O'Brien's letter of 1847 to Thomas Allsop, in The Allsop Collection, PA1680 and PA168 held at the British Library of Political and Economic Science, London

262 O'Brien, James Bronterre (2010 facsimile) p. 119; Plummer, Alfred, (1971) pp. 179-80; *Northern Star and National Trades' Journal* 24 Nov 1849 'The National Reform League'

263 Plummer, Alfred, (1971) pp. 208-9

264 in Black, F.G. and R.M. Black (eds) (1969) p. 242

265 in Plummer, Alfred, (1971) p. 173

266 Jenkins, Mick, (1980) p. 17

267 Thompson, Edward, 'The Peculiarities of the English' in Saville, John, (1987) p. 208

268 *Halifax Courier,* 6 September 1884 p. 7

269 Read, Donald, (1967) pp. 171-7; for the Reform League see Bell, Aldon D. (1961)

270 in Plummer, Alfred, (1971) p. 206

271 Patrick O'Donoghue's diary, in 'A Conspirator's Journal' on line at the National Archive of Australia, newspaper article No. 36266085

272 Jenny Mitchel letters, John Mitchel reel ZL-289, held at Manuscripts and Archives division New York Public Library

273 Forney, Gary R. (2003) p. 57-8

274 Bew, Paul, (1976) p. 246

275 *The Times* 17 Dec 1867 'Clerkenwell Explosion'

276 *The Times* 14 Dec 1867 'London'

277 *The Times* 17 Dec 1867 'Fenial Outrage'; and 'Clerkenwell Explosion'

278 *Northern Star and National Trades' Journal* 29 June 1850 'Liberation of Dr. McDouall'

279 Census Enumerator's Book: Nottingham 1861 RG 9/2457

280 for more on Feargus O'Connor's private life *see* Howe, Catherine, *Feargus O'Connor and Louisa Nisbett*

281 *Northern Star and National Trades' Journal* 26 February 1848 'To the Old Guards'

282 G.D.H. Cole traces the later middle class National Reform Union which lobbied for the Reform Act of 1867 back to Jones's Manhood Suffrage movement (Cole, G.D.H. (1941) p.352). Ernest Jones was a Vice President of the working class Reform League, which ran parallel with the middle class National Reform Union, during its existence 1865-1867.

283 *Halifax Guardian* 20 July 1850, p. 6 col.2

284 *Free Settler or Felon?* http://www.jennetwillets.com

285 Ó Broin, Leon, (1971) p. 3

286 *Cork Examiner* 12 November 1861 'Funeral Obsequies of Terence Bellew McManus'

287 in Duffy, Charles Gavan, (1883) p. 688-9n

288 *Northern Star and National Trades' Journal* 27 April 1850 'South London Chartist Hall'. 'Stone Jug' is Cockney slang for mug/fool, 'jug' is also used to mean prison.

289 Shaw, David (2008) at http://gerald-massey.org.uk/bezer/ (unpaged)

290 *Star of Freedom* 26 June 1852 'Notice!'

291 Shaw, David (2008) at http://gerald-massey.org.uk/bezer/ (unpaged)

292 *Melbourne Daily Telegraph,* 15 Oct 1875, quoted in Shaw, David (2008)

293 Thompson, Dorothy, (2015) pp. 168-71

294 Letter from Thomas Allsop to Robert Owen, 6 April 1848, held in Robert Owen Collection, Holyoake House, Manchester

295 *Northern Star and National Trades' Journal*, 15 April 1848, p.7, 'Presentation of the National Petition.'

296 Schoyen, A.R. (1958) p. 177

297 Royle, Edward, (2000), p. 84; Thompson, Dorothy (2015), p. 154; Goodway, David (1982) p. 12

298 John Bright, in referring to Ireland and the British Constitution: *There is no other country under heaven where a like state of things exists unless it be in Africa, where war and fire and capture are the fate of the weakest tribes; and all this [Ireland's condition] is under our glorious Constitution in Church and State!* (in O'Brien, R. Barry, (1910) p. 61)

299 Cooper, Thomas, (1872) (1971 edition) p. 301

300 in Goodway, (2014), p. 13

301 in Goodway, (2014), p. 11

302 in Schoyen, A.R. (1958) p. 228

303 Schoyen, A.R. (1958) p. 271

304 Aveling, Edward, in Black D. and C. Ford, (2012) p. 230-31

305 Aveling, Edward, in Black D. and C. Ford, (2012) p. 226

306 *Morning Post* 14 Dec 1897 'The Last of the Chartists'

307 *Jackson's Oxford Journal*, 5 Aug 1848 'The Rebellion in Ireland'

308 in Saville, John, (1987) p. 200

309 *Morning Chronicle* 1 Sept 1848 'The Morning Chronicle'

310 There are also parallels with the prison experiences of George Jacob Holyoake when at Gloucester gaol in 1842; also of Robert Crowe (who occupied a cell next to Ernest Jones in Tothill Bridewell in 1848). Holyoake suffered proselytisers during his time in prison and was handed a copy of William Paley's 'Evidences' by one; Crowe in his memoir mentions the building of a church and that he watched from his cell window as the spire rose up. Kingsley applies both these events to his character Alton Locke during his time in prison.

311 *see* Roberts, Stephen, (ed) (2015)

312 *Morning Post* 25 Sept 1848 'Multiple News Items'

BIBLIOGRAPHY

Central Criminal Court proceedings, **Old Bailey** on line: www.oldbaileyonline.org

Home Office papers: HO45/2410 Parts 1 and 2 held at the National Records Office, Kew

Letters:

Allsop Collection, Coll Misc. 525, held at the British Library of Political and Economic Science, London;

Robert Owen Collection held at Holyoake House, Manchester;

Letters of Queen Victoria, Vol II, p. 167, John Murray, 1908 edition;

The Harney Papers published in Black, FG & RM Black;

Jenny Mitchel letters, John Mitchel reel ZL-289, held at New York Public Library Manuscripts and Archives.

Maps: Laurie's Plan of London, Westminster & Southwark 1848 (SC/GL/FLM/051) held at the London Metropolitan Archives; Smith's New Map of London & Environs 1848 (Item Bar Code 317399-1001) held at the London Metropolitan Archives

Metropolitan Police: MEPO 2/59 held at the National Records Office, Kew

Newspapers online at British Library Papers, Gale Group database:-
Ireland: *Belfast News-Letter; The Cork Examiner; Freeman's Journal; United Irishman*
Liverpool: *Liverpool Mercury; Liverpool Times*
London: *Daily News; The Examiner; Lloyd's Weekly London Newspaper; Morning Chronicle; Morning Post; Northern Star and National Trades' Journal; The Reasoner; The Standard; Star of Freedom; The Times*
Manchester: *Chartist and Republican Journal* (held at the Working Class Library, Salford); *Manchester Times and Gazette* Newcastle: *Weekly Chronicle*

Parliamentary Debates: *Hansard* online at http://hansard.millbanksystems.com/

Shoreditch workhouse records: Feb 19 1848 microfiche X023/107 held at London Metropolitan Archives.

Treasury Solicitor reports: TS/11 held at the National Records Office, Kew

Publications

Ashton, Owen, Robert Fyson and Stephen Roberts (eds) *The Chartist Legacy*, Merlin Press (1999)

Bell, Aldon D. 'The Reform League from its origins to the Reform Act of 1867' unpublished thesis (1961), held at the Bodleian Library, Oxford

Benson, C and Viscount Esher (eds) *Letters of Queen Victoria*, Vol II, John Murray (1908)

Bew, Paul, *The Green Flag* Vol 1, Quartet Books (1976)

Black, David, 'The early Chartist and young Marx and Engels', Platypus Review issue 42, December 2011 – January 2012. https://www.internationalmarxisthumanist.org/wp-ontent/uploads/Black-Dave-Chartists-12-11.pdf

Black, F.G. & R.M. Black (eds), *The Harney Papers*, Assen (1969), held at the British Library

Blackbourn, David, *History of Germany 1780-1918*, (Second edition) Blackwell Publishing Limited (1997)

Cole, G.D.H., *Chartist Portraits*, Cassell History (1941)

Epstein, James & Dorothy Thompson (eds) *The Chartist Experience: Studies in Working-Class Radicalism and Culture, 1830-1860*, London (1982)

Forney, Gary R., *Thomas Francis Meagher: Irish Rebel, American Yankee, Montana, Pioneer,* (2003) Xlibris Corporation.

Fraser, Antonia, *Perilous Question, the drama of the Great Reform Bill 1832* Weidenfeld & Nicholson (2013)

Goodway, David, *London Chartism 1838-1848*, Cambridge University Press (1982)

Goodway, David, *George Julian Harney, The Chartists Were Right*, Merlin Press (2014)

Harte, Liam, *The Literature of the Irish in Britain*, Palgrave Macmillan (2011)

Howe, Catherine, *Halifax 1842,* Breviary Stuff Publications (2014)

Howe, Catherine, *Feargus O'Connor and Louisa Nisbett* unpublished https://www.catherinehowe.co.uk (2016)

Hoyles, Martin, *William Cuffay, the Life and Times of a Chartist Leader*, Hansib (2013)
Koseki, Takashir, *Patrick O'Higgins and Irish Chartism* held at the Working Class Movement Library, Salford, Manchester, Copy No. 36014655 Shelf Mark Ireland, Box 5
Laxton, Edward, The Famine Ships, Bloomsbury (1997 edition)
Lewis, Roy and Angus Maude, *The English Middle Classes*, Phoenix House (1949)
McCabe, Joseph, *Life and Letters of George Jacob Holyoake*, Vol I, (1908)
O'Brien, R. Barry, *John Bright, a monograph*, Smith, Elder Co. (1910)
Ó Broin, Leon, *Fenian Fever*, Chatto & Windus, (1971)
Ó Corráin, Donnchadh & Tomás O'Riordan, *Ireland 1815-1870, Emancipation, Famine and Religion*, Four Courts Press (2011)
Peacock, H.L., *A History of Modern Europe, 1789-1939*, Heinemann Educational (1958)
Pearce, Edward (ed), *The diaries of Charles Greville*, Pimlico (2006)
Percival, John, *The Great Famine, 1845-51*, BBC Books (1995)
Quennel, Peter, *Mayhew's London*, Spring Books, London
Quinault, Roland, *1848 and Parliamentary Reform, Historical Journal 31, 4* (1988)
Rapport, Mike, *1848, Year of Revolution*, Abacus (2008)
Read, Donald, *Cobden and Bright*, The Camelot Press Ltd (1967)
Read, Donald & Eric Glasgow, *Feargus O'Connor, Irishman and Chartist*, Edward Arnold Ltd (1961)
Read, Stuart J., *Lord John Russell*, (1895), The Project Gutenberg ebook edition (2008) [ebook No. 27553] online at: http://www.gutenberg.org/files/27553/27553-h/27553-h.htm
Roberts, Stephen, in Ashton, Owen, Robert Fyson and Stephen Roberts (eds) *The Chartist Legacy*, Merlin Press (1999)
Roberts, Stephen (ed) *The Dignity of Chartism*, Verso (2015)
Royle, Edward, *Radical Politics 1790-1900, Religion and Unbelief*, Longman (1971)

Royle, Edward, *Revolutionary Britannia? Reflections on the threat of revolution in Britain, 1789-1884*, Manchester University Press (2000)

Saville, John, *1848, The British state and the Chartist movement*, Cambridge University Press (1987)

Shannon, Richard, *Gladstone* Vol 1 1809-1865, Methuen, (1982)

Shaw, David, *John James Bezer Chartist and John Arnott*, (2008) online at: http://gerald-massey.org.uk/bezer/

Shoyen, A.R. *The Chartist Challenge, a portrait of George Julian Harney*, Heinemann (1958)

Thompson, Dorothy, *Outsiders*, Verso (1993)

Thompson, E.P. *The Making of the English Working Classes*, Penguin Books (1968 edition)

Townshend, Charles, *Political Violence in Ireland*, Oxford University Press (1984)

Trench, Charles Chevenix, *The Great Dan*, Jonathan Cape Ltd, (1984)

Vincent, David (ed), *Testament of Radicalism, Memoirs of Working Class Politicians 1790-1885* Europa Publications Limited (1977)

Watson, Peter, *The German Genius,* Simon & Schuster *(*2010)

Woodham-Smith, Cecil, *The Great Hunger, Ireland 1845-1849*, Penguin Books (1962 Second edition)

Wright, D.G. *The Chartist Rising in Bradford*, Bradford Libraries and Information Service (1987)

Primary Publications

Cooper, Thomas, *The Life of Thomas Cooper*, (1872), Leicester University Press 1971 edition

Crowe, Robert, *Reminiscences* on line at: babel.hathitrust.org/cgi/pt?id=mdp.39015025876833;view=1up; seq=32

Dillon, William, The Life of John Mitchel, Vol I, Kegan Paul Trench & Co., (1888) held at British Library

Doheny, Michael, *The Felon's Track or History of the Attempted Outbreak in Ireland*, (1849), W H Holbrooke, N.Y., Project Gutenberg Ebook: http://www.gutenberg.org/files/14468/14468-h/14468-h.htm

Duffy, Charles Gavan, *Four Years of Irish History, 1845-1849: A Sequel to "Young Ireland"*, Cassell, Petter, Galpin & Co., (1883), a Nabu Public Domain Reprint

Engels, Friedrich, *The Condition of the Working Class in England*, Oxford University Press (reissue 2009)

Gammage, R.G., *History of the Chartist Movement 1837-1854*, (1894) facsimile: Forgotten Books (2012)

Greville, Charles, (ed. Edward Pearce) *The Diaries of Charles Greville*, Pimlico (2006 issue)

Hollingshead, John, *Ragged London (1861)*, Everyman's Classic (1986 edition)

Jones, Ernest, *The Diary of Ernest Jones 1839-47* in 'Our History' Pamphlet 21 (1961) Self Mark A61, held at the Working Class Movement Library, Salford

Mackay Charles, *Forty Years' Recollections, of Life, Literature and Public Affairs* Chapman & Hall (1877) https://archive.org/details/fortyyearsrecoll01mackuoft

Malmesbury, *Memoirs of an Ex-Minister*, Longmans, Green & Co. (1884)

Mayhew, Henry, *The Criminal Prisons of London*, Griffin, Bohn & Company (1862)

Mayhew, Henry, in Quennel, Peter, *Mayhew's London*, Spring Books, London (undated)

McDouall, Peter, *Chartist and Republican Journal*, held at the Working Class Movement Library, Salford.

Meagher, Thomas Francis, *Memoirs of General Thomas Francis Meagher* in Cavanagh, Michael, Messenger Press (1892) http://www.archive.org/stream/memoirsgenthoma00cavagoog#page/n10/mode/2up in and in *The Tablet*, http:/archive.thetablet.co.uk

Mitchel, John, (1864), *Jail Journal, or Five years in British prison*, Sphere Books (1983 edition)

O'Brien, James Bronterre, *The Rise, Progress, and Phases of Human Slavery; How it Came into the World and How It Shall Be Made to Go Out*, Memphis, Tennessee reprint General Books (2010)

O'Donoghue, Patrick, http://trove.nla.gov.au/newspaper/article/

INDEX

Newgate prison, Dublin 49
Newgate prison, London 67, 69,
    95, 100, 113, 131, 134
Nisbett, Louisa 14, 21
Northern Star 3, 14, 15-16, 19,
    63-4, 82, 112
    Harney's editorship 17-18, 36,
        46, 120, 121
    renamed *Star of Freedom* 135

Ó Broin, Leon 132
O'Brien, James Bronterre *see*
    Bronterre O'Brien, James
O'Brien, William Smith *see* Smith
    O'Brien, William
O'Connell, Daniel 10
O'Connor, Arthur 7, 28
O'Connor, Feargus (Chartist leader)
    assassination threats 34, 36-8
    Chartist agitation and 27, 75
        National Assembly and 46, 47
        threat of force 103, 137
    Chartist Convention (1848) 29
    Chartist/Confederate alliance 9-
        10, 22-3
    class cooperation and 104, 106
    early politics 7, 9-10, 129-30
    Kennington Common 38, 39,
        40, 44, 138-9
    parliamentary speeches 44
        on 1848 petition 45
        on Irish famine 24-5
    private life 13, 14, 101, 116
        decline and death 128-9
        characteristics 9, 101, 120
    proprietorship of *Northern Star*
        17, 116
O'Mahony, John 75, 76-7, 81,
    99-100, 125-6
O'Donoghue, Patrick (Confederate)
    117, 124, 131
Old Bailey *see* London Central
    Criminal Court
Oldham 85
Owen, Robert 42

Palmerston, Lord 119
Parkhurst children 118
parliament *see* Acts of Parliament;
    British Parliament
Parliamentary and Financial
    Reform League 106
Peel, Sir Robert 10, 17
Pendegrass, Eliza 19
People's Charter and petition
    fundamental aim 130
    raising the petition 4-6
    reception by parliament 45-6
    terms are won 122-3, 144
    see also Chartists; Kennington
        Common (10th April)
People's International League 141
petition of 1848 *see* People's
    Charter and petition
Plummer, Alfred 42, 165
police *see* Birmingham Police; Irish
    Police; Metropolitan Police
Potter, Henry 54
Powell, Thomas (informer) 36, 84,
    85, 87, 91, 101
prisons *see* London prisons
Prussia 14, 17, 19, 53
Putmall, Ann 19

Reading, Thomas (informer) 36,
    71-2
Red Republican 142
Repeal Association 10
Reynolds, G.W.M. (Chartist) 27,
    29-30, 33, 40, 129, 135
Richie, Joseph (Chartist)
    arrest, trial, transportation 87,
        90-1, 100, 117, 150
    insurrectionary intent 9, 84, 85,
        86-7, 147
riots *see* London demonstrations
Roberts, W.P. 93, 115
Robertson, Matthew 61
Rowan, Charles 34, 56, 68-9, 70
Royle, Edward 141

Russell, Lord John 4, 44
  1832 Reform Bill and 103
  approach to Ireland 13, 76
  letter to Prince Albert 34
  parliamentary debates on 76
    the 1848 Chartist petition 45
    French Revolution (1848) 6
    John Mitchel's trial 50-51
    parliamentary reform 105-6
    run up to 1867 Reform Bill 122
    Chartist/Confederate view of 11,
      60, 102, 134
    views on Chartism 102, 157
  see also Whig government,
    under Russell

Saville, John i, 29
Scadding, William (Chartist)
  100-101, 113, 150
Scotland 28, 48
Sharp, Alexander (Chartist) 47, 56,
  60, 62, 139
  arrest and death in prison 67,
    97-8, 113-115, 148
Shaw, David 135-6
Shaw, John (Chartist) 47
Sheffield 97
Silesia 14
Slingsby Duncombe, Thomas 14
Smiles, Samuel 119
Smith O'Brien, William
  arrests and prosecutions 23, 80
    Clonmel trial 99, 162-3
    Dublin trial 49-50
  character 22, 77, 100, 126
    Thomas Meagher on 132-3
    views on religion 49
  Confederate Council 75
  death and legacy 132-3
  leads rebellion 76-80, 145
  Limerick speech 48-99
  parliamentary speeches
    on Irish Poor Law 24
    on Treason Felony Bill 44
  transportation 117, 124, 125

visits Paris 28
  see also Confederates
socialism 210-21
special constables 28-9, 32, 55, 57
spies 36, 71, 72, 73, 85, 91
Stanley, Lord 7
Star of Freedom 135
Stephens, James (Confederate) 75,
  80-81, 125-6, 132
strikes 9, 16-17, 97
Stuart, Lord Dudley 106

Thompson, Dorothy 137, 141
Thompson, Edward 122
Thompson, George 63
The Times 3, 33, 35, 54, 78, 90, 94,
  126-7
Tindal Atkinson 115
Tory Party 10, 17
Tothill Bridewell 27, 98-9, 113-14
Trevelyan, Charles Edward 11-12,
  76
trials 148-51
  see also individual names
Tyler family of Bethnal Green 107

Ulterior Committee conspirators
  64, 71-3, 106
  attempted rising 85-8, 140
  prominent members 84-5
United Irishman 7

Van Diemen's Land 124-5
Vernon, William John 47, 54, 55-6,
  67, 97-8, 148
Vestris, Lucy 14, 15
Victoria, Queen of England 16, 27,
  31, 34, 45, 157
  Chartist Memorial to 33, 43, 48,
    68

Wakley, Thomas 98
Walmsley, Sir Joshua 106
Walsh, Thomas (Confederate) 80
Watson, Peter 97

HISTORY, BIOGRAPHY & TRUE CRIME
FROM APS BOOKS
(www.andrewsparke.com)

Printed in Poland
by Amazon Fulfillment
Poland Sp. z o.o., Wrocław